I0100580

THE
BEHAVIORAL
HEALTH FIX

THE

BEHAVIORAL

HEALTH FIX

A Leader's Guide To Better Care, Happier
Staff, and Smoother Operations
— Without More Staff or Funding —

ISAMU PANT

Copyright © 2025 by Isamu Pant.
All rights reserved.
The Behavioral Health Fix and **Find–Fix–Serve**™ are trademarks of Isamu Pant
and may not be used without permission.

Published by **B&ILD Publishing**
Publication year: **2025**

First hardcover edition.
ISBN (Hardcover): 978-1-968627-02-7
ISBN (eBook): 978-1-968627-03-4

No part of this publication may be reproduced, stored, or transmitted in any
form or by any means without prior written permission from the author, except
for brief quotations used in reviews, academic work, or professional commentary.

Disclaimer:
This book provides educational information intended to support leadership,
operations, and organizational decision-making. It reflects the author's experience
and research. Readers should evaluate the ideas presented and apply them according to the needs and circumstances of their own organizations. The author and
publisher are not responsible for any outcomes resulting from actions taken based
on this material.

For questions, permissions, rights, or bulk orders:
support@behavioralhealthfix.com

For Becky,

You have always shown me what it looks like to do the right
thing, even when it's hard.
Your determination to leave everything better than you
found it is something I try to live up to every day.
Your unwavering support shaped the father, husband, and
leader I am today, and the one I'm still becoming.

This work is a reflection of the life you've built around us.

"Would I trust this system to take care of my daughters?"

The question that started it all.

Contents

Praise for The Behavioral Health Fix

"The Behavioral Health Fix is a refreshing, practical guide for leaders trying to navigate the chaos of today's behavioral health systems. Isamu Pant strips away jargon and complexity to deliver a clear, actionable framework—Find, Fix, Serve—that helps teams regain focus, capacity, and purpose. It's an important read for executives and clinicians who understand our current approach needs change and want real progress to create a sustainable system."

- The Honorable David J. Shulkin, M.D.
Ninth Secretary, US Department of Veterans Affairs

"As the behavioral health landscape becomes more challenging, leaders are looking for practical ways to improve organizational performance. In this book, Isamu empathetically walks leaders through a simple, repeatable process that can transform outcomes for our workforce and consumers. It's enjoyable to read and also a reference I expect to return to over and over."

- Jessica Fenchel
Chief Operations Officer, Access Services

"The Behavioral Health Fix is one of the clearest and most actionable frameworks I've encountered in my two decades in behavioral health. Isamu names what every leader feels but rarely says out loud – that burnout, turnover, and inefficiency aren't failures of people, they're failures of systems. The Find–Fix–Serve cycle is brilliant in its simplicity and powerful in its impact. This book gives leaders a way to create true relief for their teams and deliver better care without adding more work or more complexity. Our field has needed this for a long time."

- Melissa Giampietri
Executive Vice President of Behavioral Health, Clinically AI

"A great book that points out the root cause. Burnout isn't coming from our people; it's coming from the broken operational systems around them. Find–Fix–Serve gives leaders a no-excuses framework to cut the noise, fix the friction, stop normalizing dysfunction, and relieve constraints instead of pushing more work onto already stretched teams."

- Toni Baruti
CIO & CTO, AllHealth Network

"Isamu has an intimate understanding of the challenges modern behavioral-health organizations face. I've seen his work firsthand, driving meaningful outcomes across complex clinical, operational, and technology settings. His new book translates that experience into a clear, actionable framework built to create lasting, positive change."

- Mara Kailin
Chief Clinical Officer, Mind and Match

"With over 30 years across the healthcare continuum, I see the Find–Fix–Serve mechanism as a methodical way to build the muscles for continuous improvement and cultural change. Cultural change is one of the hardest things for any organization, and Find–Fix–Serve breaks it into small, measurable steps that build momentum. It delivers real outcomes within existing resources and cuts through constraints one step at a time."

- Tim Stitely
Former Chief Information Officer, U.S. Food & Drug Administration

"Isamu Pant has developed a deceptively simple yet incredibly powerful approach – Find–Fix–Serve – that helps leaders quickly identify root causes and implement sustainable improvements. Lightweight and fast, it focuses stretched teams on one core constraint at a time, turning rapid test-and-learn cycles into real relief for patients, staff, and leaders.

And while this book is written for Behavioral Health, I'm convinced the approach will work equally well in many other areas, from high tech to education, government to finance, and more."

- Simon Boothroyd

Former Global Head of Azure Services Solutions, Microsoft

How to Use This Book

This is not a book for you to read passively. It's a 30-day experiment for you to run. If you only read it, you will nod along. You will feel seen. You might even think, "We should do this someday".

But someday doesn't change anything. This system only works if you use it.

Behavioral health leaders don't need another theory of change. You have already gone through more slide decks, strategy retreats, conference sessions, and consultant workshops than you can count. What you need is something that helps you move, something that fits the realities of your organization, your staff, and the limited hours you already have.

That is what this book is written for: to help you make progress with what you already have.

The Promise

If you follow the process, you'll learn to pinpoint what's slowing your organization down, and build simple mechanisms that keep progress from slipping backward.

You'll start with insight, instead of random activity. And you'll finish with impact.

The framework you'll learn is called **Find–Fix–Serve™**. It's built around three simple questions:

1. **Find**: What's the one constraint holding us back right now?
2. **Fix**: What's the smallest test that could relieve it?
3. **Serve**: How do we make that improvement stick,

without adding more meetings or staff?

Each chapter will help you answer one of those questions.

How to Read This Book

You can approach it two ways:

→ **If you're ready to move fast**: Read the "How to" sections in Part II, and all of Chapter 7. You can read them in under 30 minutes, run the cycle with your team, and see traction within weeks.

→ **If you want lasting change**: Start at the beginning and work through each chapter. It will give you the context and the mental model that makes sustainable change. And if you want to amplify the impact, do it together with your leadership team.

The model is designed to fit inside your real schedule. You will find short stories, diagnostic questions, and tools you can use immediately. I have kept it as brief as possible without any jargon or dense theory. Just clear steps, and application.

The 30-Day Cycle

Here's how most leadership teams run the model:

Week	Focus	Action
Week 1	Find the real constraint	Define the bottleneck and align.
Week 2 – 3	Fix it with a small test	Run a test. One lever, one owner, one metric.
Week 4	Serve	Embed, scale, and decide what to test next.

At the end of each cycle, the system feels a little lighter. Teams communicate better. Meetings get shorter. And leaders reclaim hours they used to spend putting out fires.

When It Doesn't Go as Planned

Sometimes teams run the cycle and feel momentum, but not relief. That's normal. It usually means the right system is in place, but the wrong constraint was chosen. When that happens, go back to *Find*. That's where the insight lives.

If you get stuck, you will find mini FAQ's throughout Part II. They walk through the common places teams lose traction and how to course-correct.

A Final Note

Most leaders who apply this model describe the same shift: smoother operations, clearer coordination, and fewer daily breakdowns that wear teams down.

It doesn't happen overnight, but the change is real.

Use what you already have. Use it better.

And don't just read this book.

Run it.

Part I:
What's Working Against You

Every system is perfectly designed to get the results it gets.

Don Berwick

Chapter 1
Why Everything Feels Hard

Burnout isn't a personal failure. It's a systemic signal.

- Isamu Pant

You work in Behavioral Health, so you already know the weight. It's the late nights rewriting policies to meet new compliance rules. It's the open positions that stay vacant for months because talent is hard to find. It's the EHR that promised efficiency but takes fifteen clicks to do what used to take five. It's the exhaustion that sets in when even small wins feel temporary.

You don't need another white paper to tell you what's wrong. You live it everyday.

For years, this field has carried impossible loads: staff shortages, burnout, turnover, funding uncertainty, endless audits, and the constant push for "value-based outcomes." Each year brings new reforms, new systems, new expectations. Yet, somehow, it all feels the same. The people who care the most are the ones burning out the fastest.

Across the country, 90 percent of behavioral health professionals report burnout (National council for Mental Wellbeing, 2023). Direct care turnover hovers above 40 percent (Brabson et al, 2020). Medicaid, the field's main payor, rewrites the rules of engagement faster than organizations can comply. Technology vendors promise transformation, but each new platform adds another password, another report, and another workflow to maintain.

Good people aren't failing, broken systems are.

The Behavioral Health world is full of people who care. Clinicians, case managers, admin staff, IT, program directors, and everyone else, show up every day because they care. But, they're operating in systems that were never designed for the pace, the complexity, or the emotional toll of the work. Fragmented processes, outdated technology, and unclear priorities, all push caring people into burnout.

It's not because they lack resilience. It's because the system keeps demanding them to solve structural problems with personal effort. I know that world because I lived it.

When I first stepped into Behavioral Health, I wasn't coming from healthcare. I came from academia which was comfortable, predictable, and safe. I was recruited into a community behavioral health center by an executive director. They needed help using data to make decisions, which is what I did. I didn't know it then, but saying yes to that role would change everything.

Within three years, I helped build the organization's first analytics department, worked with clinical leaders in over 40 programs to redesign workflows. And I led critical strategic initiatives for the CEO that reached across the organization: clinical outcomes, staff retention, IT/Clinical coordination, EHR implementation and adoption, revenue projections, billing errors, compliance reporting, and operations. The people were extraordinary. They cared deeply and gave more than they had. But the systems? They were slowing everyone down.

Every department was doing the best it could with what it had, yet none could see the full picture. Technology didn't connect. Priorities competed instead of aligning. And leadership was over-extended, not from a lack of effort, but from the sheer noise of everything happening all at once.

When I first started at this particular organization, I thought this was just how they operated. Until I went to my first national leadership conference. That's when I realized everyone was over-extended.

I met leaders from across the country. People who loved their work and cared for their teams. And they were all saying the same thing: we don't know how to get out of this. The passion was there, but the systems were failing them. There was a sense of helplessness. And disappointingly, even the success stories on stage felt dated in terms of technology and operations. This pattern was everywhere.

A few years later, my career took me to Amazon Web Services (AWS). There, I saw a similar passion in leaders and an endless demand on their time. But the critical difference was that they had systems and structures in place. And when those didn't work, even for just a cycle, they made changes. Their passion was relentlessly accompanied by mechanisms. It wasn't about working harder; it was about working through systems that made alignment automatic.

Good intentions don't work. Mechanisms do. – Jeff Bezos

That contrast stayed with me. Behavioral Health had the people who cared, but it lacked the systems that made the work sustainable.

At AWS, I took the same systems I had put in place in Behavioral Health organizations. And I learned to refine and implement them as mechanisms at scale.

In the process, I identified why I could build departments from the ground up. Why I could successfully lead over 30 organization-wide initiatives within 4 years in Behavioral Health. Why leaders at AWS recruited me to build organization-wide KPIs. And why, 12 months later, I was asked to develop playbooks to guide work across 60 different initiatives.

Many of us get distracted by symptoms and get trapped treating the wrong problem. My superpower is to see the root cause of a problem. I am able to assess the symptoms. I can make sense of the noise. This allows me to quickly identify the actual constraint. This is why I have consistently resolved problems that leaders had been stuck with for years, in a matter of weeks. Without adding more staff or funding.

These constraints are the biggest drains to your capacity. The EHR that's burning out your clinicians is operating under fundamental constraints. The turnover in your managers and providers is because they are facing cyclical constraints. The churn in patients may be because they're facing logistic constraints.

These constraints are also why no matter how many more staff you recruit, new technology you implement, or inspiring strategic plans you write, you still don't see the difference you hope to make.

This book exists because *resolving constraints is what frees organizations.*

You don't need more people or more hours in the day. You need better mechanisms, ones that make it easier for your best people to do their best work. That's what this book will help you create.

The goal is to help leaders design organizations that finally work *for* their people, not against them.

If this feels like your day-to-day...

Scan the QR or visit
BehavioralHealthFix.com/
toolkit for a **free** 5 minute
diagnostic, and a free 30-day
planner to start relieving the
pressure in one part of your
organization.

Chapter 2
Why Our Solutions Keep Failing

Most organizations aren't failing because they're not trying. They're failing because their solutions don't target the constraint.

- Isamu Pant

The organization I'll describe here is a composite drawn from multiple behavioral health centers I've come across over the years. The patterns are real, even if the name is not.

The Cycle of False Fixes

At Good Intentions Behavioral Health, a mid-sized non-profit that serves over 16,000 patients every year, the team was doing everything "right." When burnout hit, they hired more people. When operations slowed, they bought new software. When funders demanded outcomes, they put together a new committee. Every move looked sensible on paper. Yet, six months later, the same fires burned hotter than before.

The leaders were exhausted, the staff overwhelmed, and everyone was working harder than ever. It was the same story I had seen across the board: smart, mission-driven people treating the symptoms but never the actual problem. They were stuck in endless action but little progress.

I began calling these cycles "false fixes." They're the default actions we reach for when we don't have time to pause. They feel like progress but buy only temporary relief. Each of them, like hiring more people, buying new tech, and establishing yet another committee, feeds the illusion of progress while the real constraint spreads underneath.

False Fix #1: Hire More People

Before long, the pressure to keep up with client demand made Good Intentions BH reach for the most familiar action, add more people. This was their first false fix. And it came during a staffing crisis. Caseloads had ballooned, documentation backlogs were spilling into weekends, and access times had doubled. The response was to hire more case managers.

Within three months, Good Intentions BH had added six new staff. Everyone felt hopeful. For a brief period, the load lightened. But by the end of the quarter, the documentation backlog had returned, and morale had dipped to an all-time low.

When we looked closer, things didn't add up. Each new hire took six months to onboard before reaching full productivity. Supervisors now spent most of their time training rather than leading. The EHR still required redundant entries. Every new person just multiplied the inefficiency built into the system.

This wasn't just Good Intentions BH's challenge; it reflected a national trend. Across the U.S., behavioral health clinician turnover exceeds 30 percent annually. The Health Resources and Services Administration (HRSA) projects shortages across nearly every clinical role through 2030, with psychiatrists, in particular, falling behind demand (HRSA, 2020). Hiring feels productive, but in a system full of friction, adding people slows things down more, and rarely has the intended outcome.

In many instances, the real issue isn't capacity. Good Intentions BH didn't need more people. They needed to make it easier for their people to succeed.

Research supports this: studies in hospital and health systems have shown that adding staff, alone, rarely improves outcomes or efficiency. In one study, increasing physician numbers did not enhance quality of care (McCarthy, 2016). Other studies of care coordination found that when systems are inefficient, more staff simply multiply hand-offs and administrative load rather than reduce it (Wager et al., 2019).

The real leverage comes from clarity and structure, not headcount. The signal from the field is consistent: administrative layers grow, care time shrinks, and staff exhaustion deepens.

When the structure has embedded friction, more people just intensify it.

Good Intentions BH learned that lesson. Six months later, they weren't talking about hiring; they were talking about surviving. Which led to the next fix.

False Fix #2: Buy New Technology

When the documentation backlog continued to grow, even with additional staff, leadership turned to technology. Vendors pitched software promising automation, compliance tracking, and reduced workload. The demos were impressive, with dashboards full of data and elegant workflows. It felt perfect.

They purchased a new EHR, and a separate project management tool to track the implementation. Implementation took nine months, overlapping with grant reporting season. But the EHR wasn't set up for grant reporting, so staff had to enter data into two different systems. Efficiency plummeted. Meetings doubled. By the time the system stabilized, frontline staff were begging for paper forms just to keep pace with patients.

A 2025 review found that EHR usability issues directly contribute to workflow disruption and documentation burden, exactly what staff at Good Intentions BH's were feeling (Olakotan et al., 2025). When technology is introduced without resolving operational issues, it adds to existing noise and amplifies change fatigue. Yet, when technology is anchored to a specific constraint, it can drive outcomes. A recent multisite study found ambient scribing and AI-assisted documentation can measurably reduce burnout and charting time (You et al., 2025).

One challenge is that EHR's were not originally designed for Behavioral Health organizations. The 2009 federal HITECH incentives fueled EHR adoption in hospitals, but excluded behvioral health organizations. So most systems were retrofits and not purpose-built. Studies show that while 84 percent of behavioral health facilities now use electronic records, adoption varies widely, with some under 60 percent (HRSA, 2024).

This has created workaround measures that complicate daily workflows. These workflows get mapped into new technology. And the constraints live on. Only now, it is even messier than before.

At Good Intentions BH, team meetings were tense. Clinicians were constantly frustrated. The regularly shared that they didn't get into behavioral health to spend all day clicking check-boxes and entering data. They weren't being cynical. They were just tired. Tired of technology that distanced them from their patients.

Technology amplifies whatever baseline it enters: outcomes or noise.

False Fix #3: Form Another Committee

The third fix arrived inspired by a board retreat. Leadership was eager to "realign strategy with execution." So, they announced the formation of a cross-functional committee. The idea was simple: bring together leaders from across programs to solve issues that had resurfaced over the past year.

It sounded promising. Committees are the safe bet when things feel stuck. No one can argue with collaboration. So the leadership put together a 12 person committee. It started strong with a list of issues. But they didn't have enough information to prioritize: Which issue was more immediate? How would they decide which one to solve? Or how to solve it? No one was certain, and loudest voices started getting traction.

Within weeks, enthusiasm began to fade. The group met regularly but struggled to define its purpose. Agendas blurred between operational updates and strategic brainstorms. Decisions rarely stuck, because the committee had no real authority to implement change.

Across Good Intentions BH, clinicians described being "voluntold" into committees. They met often, decided little, and drained energy from patient care. Management research echoes this frustration. Excessive committees and touch points create collaborative overload. Burnout rises while output drops (Cross et al., 2016). Despite more dashboards and meetings, leaders often miss the few signals that matter (Shapiro, 2017).

For front line staff, creating committees became a ritual. Meetings filled with everyone talking about the problem, but no one with the bandwidth or clarity to fix it. For leadership, it created the illusion of momentum without the mechanisms to sustain it.

This is common practice across behavioral health and human services. Committees are formed to address crises, pilot improvements, or satisfy funders demanding "collaborative oversight." But most of these groups don't create real movement. They meet, discuss, request more data, revisit the same issues, and then schedule another meeting. The problem isn't effort, it's structure. Without clear decision rights, ownership, or accountability, committees become conversation loops instead of engines of change. And the longer this goes on, the more time gets drained from actual improvement work.

You can't organize your way out of unclear priorities.

By this point, leaders at Good Intentions BH's were drained. They had hired staff, invested in technology, and assembled committees. But the fires still burned. Everyone was working hard but nothing fundamental had changed.

Why Consultants & Frameworks Often Miss the Mark

Some other common fixes include hiring consultants and using different frameworks.

Consultants usually arrive with full toolkits: EOS, Lean, Agile, assessments, reorg kits, and best practices. But often, they leave behind more noise than clarity. It's not because they lack ability; it's because most frameworks assume a baseline of stability, clarity, and control. And behavioral health systems rarely have those.

In highly-controlled corporate settings, frameworks shine. But in a field with fluctuating funding, staff turnover, crisis workflows, and compliance shocks, the context wins. Implementation science research supports this. Even with detailed planning, interventions frequently fail because of contextual factors (e.g., culture, workflows, and underlying incentives) (Damschroder et al., 2022). The very assumptions that frameworks rely on is their blind spot. When ideals are forced into a messy reality, it costs time, focus, and goodwill. That's the unseen cost. Consultants drain organizational energy to drive frameworks, rather than frameworks energizing the organization.

At Good Intentions BH, implementing the EOS framework became a project unto itself. Silos formed around choosing template language, conducting readiness interviews, customizing reports. Months later, leaders looked around wondering why nothing had changed. Hundreds of hours spent in meetings, creating documentation, and building staff buy-in. That is the cost of misapplied structure.

So in this book, we don't start with frameworks or consultants. We start with the constraint. Because frameworks are most effective when pointed at the root cause, and not the symptoms.

The Pattern Beneath Them

The same pattern runs through every false fix: effort is never the issue. The system keeps treating the symptoms instead of root causes.

If effort isn't the issue, the question becomes: what is really slowing us down?

That's what we turn to next.

Tired of fixes that don't stick?

Scan the QR or visit BehavioralHealthFix.com/ toolkit for a **free** diagnostic that shows where your organization is leaning on "false fixes" instead of addressing the real constraint.

Chapter 3
The Real Constraint

A system is never the sum of its parts. It's the product of their interactions.

Peter Senge

If you lead a behavioral health organization, you've probably felt it, the constant push and pull between compassion and capacity. You're trying to do good work in a system that's always one staff resignation, one funding change, or one tech update away from breaking. And yet, every time something breaks, the reflex is the same:

- "We need more people."
- "We need a better system."
- "We need more money."

But what if those aren't the real problems? What if the true barrier to progress isn't *how much* you have, but *where* you're constrained?

Why Behavioral Health Feels Hard Right Now

Across the United States, behavioral health leaders are fighting fires on all sides. The shortage data alone is staggering:

- Over 122 million Americans now live in a designated Mental Health Professional Shortage Area (HRSA, 2024).
- Nearly 93 percent of behavioral health workers report experiencing burnout, with 62% describing it as moderate to severe (NCMW, 2023).
- Turnover rates in community behavioral health average 30–40 percent annually, and the pipeline of licensed professionals is far behind demand (HRSA, 2024).

That's before factoring in administrative load, compliance pressure, and technology friction, the invisible forces that drain hours and morale. The Centers for Disease Control and Prevention found that poor work conditions and insufficient time to finish work were among the strongest predictors of burnout among health workers (Nigam, 2023).

In short, this is not a people problem. It's a systems problem. When operations are out of sync, the system derails even the most dedicated staff.

"A bad system will beat a good person every time."
- W. Edwards Deming

These pressures have pushed leaders into survival mode. Teams are reactive instead of strategic. Projects compete instead of connect. And staff feel like they're constantly running but not moving forward. This exhaustion creates a false sense of "we just need more capacity." But as we'll see, adding capacity without alignment often makes things worse.

The Three Universal Constraints

Every organization, from startups to state agencies, runs on the same triad: People, Process, and Technology. If your organization feels stuck, one of these is holding you back right now:

→ **People** – Skill gaps, role confusion, burnout, turnover, or cultural friction.

→ **Process** – Bottlenecks, rework, excessive approvals, misaligned priorities, poor data flow.

→ **Technology** – Systems that don't talk, data buried in reports, tools implemented before workflows are clear.

You may recognize you currently have more than one constrained area. Most organizations have constraints in each of these. But here's the truth:

Only one of them is the biggest constraint: the area creating the greatest bottleneck right now. The others are symptoms.

If you don't find it, you'll keep fixing the wrong thing,

and making the right people miserable in the process.

The Staffing Crisis That Wasn't About Staffing

Intake at Good Intentions BH had been under strain for months. Two of the six intake coordinators resigned within a short window, and the remaining team was overwhelmed.

To keep access open, the COO reassigned eight staff from other departments to rotate through intake a couple of days each week. On paper, the redistribution seemed reasonable. In practice, it created new problems almost immediately: inconsistent workflows, higher error rates, and a group of already stretched staff now juggling two jobs. By the end of the month, burnout had spread across three departments.

Inside the organization, the working theory was simple: *"We're understaffed. This is just the new normal."* Morale boosters like pizza lunches, small bonuses, pep talks were rolled out, but nothing meaningfully changed. Vacancies went unfilled. Access bottlenecks grew. Documentation lagged.

For almost two years, the data had been signaling strain across the system: clinician overload, documentation delays, longer wait times, and inconsistent billing capture. The COO had surfaced this repeatedly, but each attempt to act stalled amid competing priorities.

At first glance, it looked like a textbook capacity issue. The COO felt as if the organization and the rest of the leadership just didn't care enough. But it wasn't due to apathy or resistance. The organization had too many fires to put out, and too many disconnected initiatives to manage.

When the leadership team finally took a constraint diagnostic together, a different pattern emerged. Their challenges weren't rooted in staffing at all. Underneath everything was a decision bottleneck.

The following day, the team met to address alignment directly. Together, they created a lightweight decision framework grounded in their mission, their values, and a small set of operating principles. A simple method to determine what gets attention, why, and when.

They pressure tested the framework by sifting through a long list of priorities: EHR upgrades, audit prep, supervisor turnover, documentation targets, crisis response, and intake volume.

Within two weeks, they used the same framework to decide where to reallocate limited hiring resources, how to better support clinical managers, and how to increase retention. Redundant approvals were removed, and responsibility was clarified. No new funding. No reorganization. Just clear responsibilities and shared accountability.

And as it almost always happens when you fix the true constraint, it amplified progress across multiple fronts at Good Intentions BH.

It's also the lesson that frames this entire chapter: when you chase symptoms, you create complexity. When you name the constraint, you can finally make progress and provide relief.

Why Drag and Drop Frameworks Keep Failing

Behavioral health has borrowed many frameworks from business and healthcare improvement movements: Lean, Agile, Six Sigma, EOS, PDSA, Waterfall, and others. You have probably at least heard of, if not used some of these. Each promised efficiency and accountability. Few delivered it.

The reason is context. These frameworks are powerful in stable, resource-rich environments. But behavioral health operates in the opposite: unpredictable demand, chronic underfunding, and workforce turnover that resets institutional memory every few years. The result? Leaders spend more time maintaining the systems than fixing the problem.

Before we throw them out entirely, let's look at where they fall short, and what makes them valuable once adapted.

<u>Lean: Built for factories, not funding cycles</u>

Lean was designed to eliminate waste and improve flow. In manufacturing, where variables are controlled and demand is predictable, it thrives. But behavioral health is unpredictable. Demand spikes, patients cancel, funding shifts, and documentation rules evolve.

Lean often adds extra measurement systems, facilitators, and training layers that small agencies can't sustain. A 2023 review of Lean in healthcare found many initiatives were either superficial or failed to sustain beyond the pilot phase (Wager et al., 2022). Staff reported fatigue from meetings and operational metrics that didn't reflect their daily reality.

Agile: Great in theory, difficult to implement

Agile methods (like Scrum or Kanban) emphasize short cycles and empowered teams. But in clinical operations, compliance and risk limit autonomy. A therapist can't "iterate" mid-treatment plan or skip documentation for speed. Plus for these approaches to work, they need strong philosophical underpinnings that require significant training and coaching. Without adaptation, Agile becomes an appealing way to hide existing dysfunctions.

EOS: Entrepreneurial focus, clinical blind spots

The Entrepreneurial Operating System (EOS) brings helpful structures such as vision, scorecards, and weekly meetings. But in mission-driven organizations, EOS adds meeting overhead and metrics management without addressing systemic friction. EOS assumes stable roles and commercial incentives, two things behavioral health rarely has.

Quality Improvement & PDSA: Incrementalism in a crisis environment

Plan-Do-Study-Act cycles and Six Sigma offer rigor, but they depend on analytic infrastructure and stable conditions. Most community providers don't have the data or resources to run controlled experiments. So, improvement fatigue and data overload can easily undermine sustainability.

Waterfall: Predictable only on paper

Traditional project management thrives on predictability

with milestones, gates, and deliverables. Behavioral health programs live in constant adaptation. By the time a Gantt chart is finalized, the grant requirements have already changed. The result across all these frameworks is the same: more process, more meetings, more personnel, and no lasting improvement.

Culture eats strategy for breakfast. - Peter Drucker

These imported frameworks assume stability, capacity, and discretionary time, which are all luxuries that behavioral health doesn't have. When you drop these frameworks into an exhausted environment, you're asking an overworked staff to change their habits *and* manage a new process on top of it. That's not improvement, it's overload.

What's missing is the diagnostic step. The pause to ask: Where is the real constraint? Without it, these frameworks become a crutch, nothing more than a prop. With it, they become leverage.

Why These Frameworks Still Matter

Before you throw out these frameworks entirely, it's worth remembering that each one was built to solve a real problem. There's still value in them if you know when and how to apply their best parts. But only when adapted.

None of these systems are inherently wrong. In fact, there are powerful learnings, and my work has incorporated many of their core principles. They're just incomplete when applied to behavioral health as is. Each has a valuable lens:

→ **Lean** teaches flow and waste elimination.

→ **Agile** reinforces iteration and staff empowerment.

→ **EOS** encourages leadership rhythm and accountability.

→ **PDSA** drives disciplined learning.

→ **Waterfall** adds structure for predictable projects.

The problem is *sequencing*. Leaders often layer frameworks before fixing the constraint. That's like installing new plumbing without checking where the blockage is.

When you find the real constraint (people, process, or tech), then and only then, can you pull the right piece from each framework to strengthen that area. That's the essence of constraint-based operations. It's not about rejecting established frameworks; it's about leveraging them correctly.

The Meta-Constraint

If you've been through any change initiative, you know this truth: nothing sticks without alignment. Alignment doesn't mean universal agreement. It means a shared understanding that drives action towards the desired change. When leaders aren't aligned:

• Departments optimize for their own metrics at the cost of collaboration.

• Initiatives compete for the same staff time.

• Front-line workers receive conflicting directives.

In that environment, even the best frameworks will fail.

In behavioral health, misaligned paradigms such as clinical vs. operational, and mission vs. margin create invisible drag.

At Good Intentions BH, the leadership team had decided to streamline operations across a grant-funded program. But each leader involved had a different view of what 'success' meant: one focused on compliance, another on patient satisfaction, and the third on staff well-being.

The result was that they weren't able to make any progress. Until they had help aligning those priorities into a shared definition of success, no process change would hold. Once leaders were aligned, operational friction dropped and staff engagement rose within a single quarter.

Peter Senge called this the tragedy of the unshared mental model (Senge, 1990). When you align leadership around the real constraint, energy stops scattering. Communication sharpens. Teams recover focus. Progress accelerates.

The Three Tests

Now that we've identified why frameworks can fail and why alignment matters, let's move from concept to application. These tests mark the first practical move into the Find-Fix-Serve framework, your personal toolkit to spot where your constraint hides and leverage begins.

Here's a simple way to start diagnosing where your constraint lives:

1) People Test
   Ask: Are we losing good staff faster than we can replace them? Are roles clear, supported, and pro-

tected from chaos? If not, your constraint might be People.

2) Process Test

   Ask: Where does work stall? Which meetings or approvals drain more energy than they create? Where do priorities collide? If you can't visualize your workflow, your constraint is likely Process.

3) Technology Test

   Ask: How much time is spent double-entering, reconciling, or searching for data? How many tools do you have that nobody fully trusts? If staff are adapting to tech instead of tech adapting to them, your constraint is likely Technology.

These three questions are foundational for operational clarity. Everything we've discussed so far, the drag of misapplied frameworks, the power of alignment, and the clarity these three tests bring set the stage for what comes next. The next step is where theory meets implementation.

The Find-Fix-Serve Framework

This is the operating flywheel I use in every engagement, whether it's a community agency, a startup, or a corporation:

→ **Find** – Locate the real constraint (People, Process, or Technology). Use diagnostics, interviews, or even just a whiteboard conversation to expose where friction lives.

→ **Fix** – Simplify it with the lightest possible mechanism. Remove one approval, clarify one role, retire one redundant report. Do less, better.

→ **Serve** – Reinforce the new Fix with rhythm and accountability. Serve your staff by giving them clear expectations and breathing room. Serve your patients by ensuring continuity and quality. Serve your mission by protecting what works.

When you move through these three steps, everything else begins to fall into place. Burnout drops. Throughput rises. Leaders spend less time managing crises and more time leading.

This is operational clarity: the moment when systems serve people, not the other way around.

Why This Works When Others Didn't

Constraint-based thinking isn't new. Goldratt's *Theory of Constraints* has been around for decades. But behavioral health has never fully embraced it, maybe because of cultural resistance to business language. Yet, many enduring practices, from Amazon's "Invent and Simplify" principle to the CDC's emergency response playbooks, run on constraint discipline. They focus effort where it matters most.

Edward Deming, Eliyahu Goldratt, and Peter Drucker all warned against confusing activity with impact. Behavioral scientists like BJ Fogg, James Clear, and Daniel Kahneman later showed why: humans resist change when systems make it hard to see progress.

That's why you can't drag-and-drop industrial frameworks into human services. You must adapt frameworks to human energy, the scarcest resource of all.

When you apply Find – Fix – Serve, you reduce friction before adding force. And then you *Serve* by reinforcing what works. Service isn't just about patient care; it's about empowering your people through clarity, your teams through rhythm, and your mission through focus. It's how operational systems become acts of care, and move beyond just tracking productivity. Staff finally feel supported instead of managed.

"Simplicity is the ultimate sophistication." - Leonardo da Vinci

From Constraint to Progress

When behavioral health organizations find and fix their real constraint, remarkable things start to happen:

→   Staff rediscover purpose.

→   Leadership regains time.

→   Patients experience smoother care.

→   Data tells the same story across departments.

Progress doesn't come from doing more. It comes from doing the *right* thing next. The frameworks that failed before, Lean, Agile, EOS, suddenly start to work because the foundation underneath them is healthy. They stop adding friction and start amplifying outcomes.

That's the promise of constraint-based problem solving: when you design around what limits you most, everything else accelerates.

From Diagnosis to Design

Every leader in this field cares deeply. No one shows up to work in behavioral health for fame or fortune. They show up to make a difference. And they stay, even when the system makes that harder every year.

But compassion needs structure. Purpose needs process. Leadership needs results. If you remember one thing from this chapter, let it be this: **you can't fully serve your mission until you've fixed your constraint.**

Find where the friction is. Fix it with simplicity. Serve through it with alignment and rhythm. Once your operations stop breaking your people, your people will start transforming your outcomes. That's where we go next.

"Vision without systems is fantasy. Systems without vision is bureaucracy."

Find your real constraint in 5 minutes.

Scan the QR or visit
BehavioralHealthFix.com/
toolkit to take a **free** Find–
Fix–Serve™ diagnostic, and
identify the one bottleneck
that will move everything else.

Part II:

The Way Out

You do not rise to the level of your goals. You fall to the level of your systems.

James Clear

Chapter 4
FIND the Constraint

There is nothing so useless as doing efficiently that which should not be done at all.

Peter Drucker

Think back to the last time you needed care, any kind of care, and you had to wait. You called a clinic for an appointment and were told, "Earliest we can get you in is three weeks." So you counted down the days waiting to get the care you needed. When the day finally arrived, you sat in a waiting room, watching staff shuffle papers, apologizing for the delay with tired smiles. You know the staff are trying their best, but it didn't change your experience.

You've felt that frustration as a patient. And here you are leading that very system, trying so hard to change that experience for your staff and your patients. You've pushed for better workflows, new tools, more alignment, but the same friction returns. It's exhausting, isn't it? You turn over one problem, just to find another hiding under it.

Behind every waiting patient is a clinician waiting too, for approvals, signatures, data, and systems to load. Or a front desk staff trying to work with tools that always take too much time. Each delay ripples through your organization as lost hours, frustrated staff, and missed opportunities for care.

The Hidden Drain You Don't See

How many new patients did you intake this week? Do you have a waitlist you can't keep up with? Or are you struggling to maintain enough volume to stay sustainable?

Each intake takes hours: gathering data, entering it into multiple systems, verifying coverage, collecting consents, scheduling, and documentation.

According to the Colorado Behavioral Healthcare Council (2020), the average behavioral health intake consumes 2–4 hours of staff time *before a single session occurs.* Multiply that across your caseload, and the friction becomes staggering.

Let's do the math:
- 25 new intakes per week × 3 hours each = 75 staff hours per week
- ≈ 300 hours per month (almost two full workweeks)
- ≈ 3,600 hours per year
- At $30/hour, that's $108,000 in annual capacity lost

That's time and energy that could be spent on direct care, follow-ups, or staff wellbeing.

Now imagine cutting that burden in half through constraint-focused redesign. Simplified forms, clearer ownership, or improved automation:

- 1,800 hours reclaimed annually
- Equivalent to one full-time staff position
- Potential reinvestment: patient sessions, outreach, care coordination, or staff relief

The ROI is immediate. Every hour reclaimed allows you to serve more patients or reinvest in staff support.

The Rising Stakes

If a patient in need has to choose between a tech-first behavioral health startup promising same-day appointments from home, or a 2 week wait to be seen at Good Intentions BH, which would they choose?

Which would YOU choose?

Even if that service doesn't offer the same depth or whole-person care you provide, the perception of speed and ease is powerful. As McKinsey & Company (2023) reports, patients increasingly expect behavioral health services to be available on demand, emphasizing immediacy and convenience over traditional scheduling.

If your intake still takes weeks, you're not just losing time, you're losing trust, patients, and relevance. But you know this already.

What the Competition Really Solved

Tech-first startups like Talkspace, Cerebral and Headway didn't invent new types of therapy. They simply *removed friction.* They automated scheduling, removed documentation loops, and connected waiting patients with available clinicians in a fraction of the time traditional systems allowed.

These companies succeeded not because they revolutionized care, but because they targeted the very constraints that older systems treated as the norm. As Reilly (2023) noted, the behavioral-health ecosystem remains "out of alignment" because the flow between demand and supply isn't yet frictionless. Meanwhile, Truong's review (2022) of digital mental-health platforms found that top enterprises all emphasized on-demand consultation rather than novel therapeutic modalities.

That's the real story behind their growth. It wasn't technology for its own sake. It was constraint-elimination wrapped in technology.

These platforms focused on rapid provider-matching and scheduling, replacing week-long delays with same-day or next-day access (Truong, 2022). They replaced multiple intake steps, redundant paperwork, and long waits with simple, streamlined workflows designed around the patient.

These aren't breakthroughs in treatment. They're what happens when you remove friction:

→ Instant scheduling
→ Streamlined onboarding

→ Fewer intake hoops

The technology is just the wrapper. The engine underneath is constraint-clarity.

The next evolution of behavioral health won't come from bigger software budgets. It will come from leaders who learn to *Find* and *Fix* the real bottlenecks that technology has only managed to hide.

Why "We've Tried Everything" Still Feels Stuck

When outcomes stall, leaders often double down on effort. But more effort isn't the answer when operations itself is blocking flow.

The U.S. Department of Veterans Affairs learned this firsthand. Facing public outrage over appointment backlogs, the VA invested millions to reduce patient wait times to 14 days. They hired more staff, added call centers, and revamped scheduling systems. Even still many facilities remained gridlocked.

The root issue? Scheduling complexity and role confusion. Administrative staff, clinicians, and managers each optimized their own part, but those parts didn't align. The result was friction everywhere (Harvard Business Review, 2016).

When they finally approached the problem as a constraint, redesigning the workflow, clarifying decision rights, and embedding cross-team coordination, throughput improved dramatically.

- Fewer patients waited.
- Staff felt less pressure.

- Leaders finally had space to think long-term.

You can probably see yourself in that story. The spreadsheets. The late-night emails. The consultants promising transformation in 6 months. The relief when something *finally* starts to work.

The lesson is simple: until you find the true constraint, every fix is a guess.

The Find–Fix–Serve™ Loop (Your Operating Rhythm)

Most leaders don't need more motivation. They need a map. The Find–Fix–Serve™ loop is that map: a way to locate friction, act on it, and free your organization to do what matters most. To serve.

→ **Find**: Identify the highest-leverage constraint, the one point where friction blocks progress.

→ **Fix**: Apply focused effort and a small test to relieve that constraint.

→ **Serve**: Deliver greater value to both patients and staff, the two sides of your mission.

When this loop is working, it becomes self-reinforcing. Fixing a bottleneck in patient flow helps clinicians reclaim time and energy. That energy improves care and morale, which stabilizes funding and staffing. It's not about squeezing productivity. It's about building resilience and capacity.

This is what makes behavioral health different. We don't Find and Fix to grow profit. We Find and Fix to serve more, and protect the people doing the hardest work.

Recent research in behavioral health makes this connection explicit: workforce well-being directly influences both patient outcomes and staff retention. Hallett et al. (2023) found that stress, burnout, and lack of organizational support were major drivers of turnover in public behavioral health systems, the same conditions that erode consistency and continuity of care.

In other words, serve has two inseparable components:

- **Patients**: Outcomes depend on reliable access and continuity of care.
- **People**: Well-being determines whether that care is sustainable.

The loop isn't abstract. It's how you turn daily complexity into steady outcomes.

Why FINDing Is Hard

Finding sounds simple, but in practice it's the hardest part. Here's why leaders miss it:

1) Too Much Data, Too Little Signal: Dashboards multiply faster than decisions. Metrics describe what's happening, not why. Reports arrive two weeks late, and everyone argues about whose numbers are right.

2) Competing Priorities: Every team's issue feels urgent. Planning sessions sound like echo chambers of what funders, peers, or think tanks say is strategic. You pick safe goals that look good on paper but don't reflect your reality.

3) Adaptive Workarounds: Your best people are your

best firefighters. They create spreadsheets to patch software, memorize workarounds, and carry the burden of keeping things running. They're brilliant, and they're exhausted.

4) Psychological Distance: You see the numbers, high demand, low utilization, and assume people aren't working efficiently. But spend a day in the clinic, and you'll see clinicians buried under redundant documentation and hand offs that stall patient care. Staff don't speak up because dashboards show pressure without context. They worry that sharing what's not working will be seen as resistance, not insight. The right signals never surface, and well-intentioned initiatives pile up without relieving strain.

How to FIND the actual problem

If you take one thing from this chapter, make it this section. The Find Mechanism gives you a repeatable way to diagnose and fix what's slowing you down in one focused session.

You'll know it worked if everyone leaves with one clear sentence:

"We can't _____ because _____."

Step 1: Start with the Symptom (15 min)

Ask:

1) What's the problem keeping us up right now?
2) How does it show up day-to-day for staff or patients?
3) What have we already tried, and what happened?

Keep it concrete. Capture 3–5 specific pains, short phrases like waitlist, turnover, billing backlog. Don't rush to data yet. Honor the lived frustration first.

Step 2: Quantify the Friction (20 min)

Turn emotion into signals.

Ask:

1) How often does this happen?
2) How much time, money, or energy does it cost weekly?
3) Who else feels the impact? Patients, clinicians, admin?
4) If nothing changed for 90 days, what would that mean for care or morale?

Estimate roughly. Direction beats precision. Rank each by impact: High / Medium / Low.

Step 3: Map the Interconnections (30 min)

Every visible pain usually hides a web of invisible problems.

Ask:

1) What does this pain depend on?
2) Where does the handoff or delay actually happen?
3) If this improved, which other problems would ease up?

Draw arrows between problems. The nodes connecting multiple problems likely reveals your constraint, and your point of leverage.

Step 4: Name the Constraint (20 min)

Move from discussion to definition.

Ask:

1) If we fixed one thing and nothing else, which would free up the most progress?
2) Is this mainly a People, Process, or Technology issue?
3) Can we say it in one sentence that a new hire would understand?"

Example: We can't schedule faster because our intake team re-enters data twice.

Assign ownership and define success in 30 days. Write that sentence in bold, your **Named Constraint**.

Step 5: Close the Loop (10 min)

Turn this FIND into commitment.

Ask:

1) Who understands best how this works every day?
2) Who else can help us think about potential solutions, especially unconventional ones?
3) When can we all meet in the next 3 days to work on this?

Set a meeting date before you leave the room. You have uncovered the constraint, but this is just the starting point.

Example:

- Symptom: "Our wait-list is too long."
- Statement: *We can't reduce wait times because scheduling is manual and fragmented*
- Quantified: Average = 18 days to first appointment.
- Mapped: Intake → Scheduling → Clinician assignment → First session.
- Constraint: Scheduling backlog — one staff member manually calls every patient.

The Simpler Lens – People, Process, Technology

You'll notice most constraints fall into one of three categories:

→ **People**: clarity, communication, capacity.
→ **Process**: duplication, hand-offs, feedback loops.
→ **Technology**: tools that add work instead of removing it.

You don't need to diagnose them perfectly, just recognize which one is blocking flow the most. That's enough to start.

Mini-FAQ: Your First Questions About FIND

What if we pick the wrong constraint?
That's fine. The cost of one short Find session is small compared to a six-month strategic miss. If it doesn't relieve pressure, you've learned quickly and can rerun it with better insight.

What if staff are too busy to sit in another meeting?
Then FIND is exactly what they need. The goal is to reduce the noise that's stealing their time. If your team leaves with one actionable sentence, "We can't __ because __", they've bought back hours already.

What if the real problem is outside our control?
Perfect. That's information you can act on. Find distinguishes internal from external friction, so you stop wasting effort on what you can't move yet, and double down on what you can.

What if leadership wants proof before trying this?
Reframe it: you're not spending time, you're buying *clarity*. A one-hour diagnostic that prevents an unproductive initiative is a great ROI for leadership.

What Happens Next

After two or three successful cycles, you'll begin to notice patterns, how the same constraint themes keep resurfacing across teams.

That's when you're ready for the system-level version of

Find: mapping how your entire organization creates, transfers, and loses momentum. It's a powerful space to be in, but out of scope for this book.

Closing Reflections – Seeing Changes Everything

Finding the constraint isn't glamorous. It rarely shows up in reports. But once you see it, truly see it, you'll never lead the same way again. Most leaders spend their careers fixing symptoms. The few who master this constraint-loop fix systems.

That's where transformation begins. Once you know what's slowing you down, everything you do next compounds.

In the next chapter, we'll move to **Fix**, the art of addressing that constraint, and **Serve,** redesigning your organization for sustainable flow. You'll see how to run focused change in 30-day bursts. You will then embed those bursts into your existing operating rhythm in Chapter 9, so the loop becomes your organizational culture.

FIND your real constraint in 5 minutes.

Scan the QR or visit
BehavioralHealthFix.com/
toolkit for a **free** 5 min
diagnostic to Find your
constraint, and see what's
really slowing you down.

Chapter 5
FIX the Constraint

Give me a lever long enough, and I can move the world.

- Archimedes

Have you ever been here? You finally secure a new grant, launch a "Transformation Initiative", or roll out a big, new software platform, and instead of things getting lighter, they somehow get heavier.

Meetings multiply. Staff feel more confused than energized. The promise of transformation turns into months of extra work and re-training. Patients are waiting, teams are still tired, and you're left with another round of change fatigue.

If that sounds familiar, you're not alone.

The Common Pattern

Every year, leaders across healthcare and behavioral health

invest millions into major initiatives meant to solve chronic problems:

- New EHR systems that were supposed to integrate care, but added extra steps instead.
- Lean Six Sigma projects aimed at driving efficiency, but never made it past the pilot phase.
- Cross-team collaborations designed to improve patient support, but left the same few high performers doing even more.

These efforts often start with optimism and a strong case for change. A consultant's slide deck paints the vision; staff nod along. But then the roll-out begins. A manager pulls you aside: "We can't find coverage to attend the next training." Someone on the team asks, "Will this change how we bill?" Suddenly, what looked like alignment starts to splinter into confusion. And recent studies reflect this:

- McKinsey & Company (2021) found that nearly 70 percent of large-scale transformations fail to meet their goals. This often happens because employee-resistance and weak managerial support undermine efforts before the new systems stabilize.
- Gallup (2025) reported the steepest drop in employee engagement since the pandemic. It was largely driven by exhausted managers navigating "disruption at every level," from restructuring to AI-driven workload expansion.

So if you've ever felt like your improvement initiative made things worse before they got better, you're not alone.

Research from McKinsey & Company and Creasey(2025) reinforce that major change initiatives almost always trigger a short-term decline in performance or productivity, often 20–30 percent, as staff adapt to new workflows and expectations.

Why Big Change Fails in Behavioral Health

Behavioral health systems operate under chronic constraint: limited funding, staff shortages, and constant regulatory shifts. Every large-scale initiative competes with day-to-day survival. While a Fortune 500 company can afford 18 months of change management, staff in behavioral health organization are juggling crisis calls, audits, and staff turnover everyday.

That's why major change initiatives in behavioral health seem to collapse under their own weight. The plans and assumptions are too detached from the realities of the day to day operations. They assume stability that doesn't exist.

In contrast, smaller, contained tests work with your constraints instead of against them. Camilleri et.al.(2019) found that organizations attempting large-scale changes experience significantly higher rates of change fatigue, than those adopting smaller rollouts released in phases to test, then scale.

The Better Way: Micro-Fixes That Move Fast

Instead of launching another major change initiative, what if you tried a two-week experiment? Not a full roll-out, just a focused test.

Small, fast experiments are how progress happens rapidly inside complex, capacity-strained systems. You learn quickly, reduce risk, and, most importantly, show your team that change can make life easier, not harder.

At Good Intentions BH, they had chronic friction between IT and clinical operations. Clinical leaders would ask for simple reports, and tweaks to forms in the EHR. But IT never seemed to have the time for it. Everything stayed as an unresolved ticket. Meanwhile, IT was working overtime untangling software built on workarounds.

Both sides were frustrated. Requests had piled up for months with little communication. Tired of the friction someone proposed a committee to replace the ticketing system. Thankfully, instead of a six-month technology overhaul, they started Find. They found the key constraint was actually a lack of shared prioritization. The Fix? A single weekly 10 minute "ops huddle" between the IT lead and a clinical supervisor.

Within three weeks, 70% of pending tickets were either resolved or clarified. No new software. No new staff. No new metrics. No new committee. Just a lever tested, measured, and proven. That's what this chapter is about.

Mini-FAQ: Your First Objections

What if we pick the wrong lever?
That's fine. The cost of a 2-week test is tiny compared to the cost of a failed roll-out. If it doesn't relieve the constraint, you've learned a critical lesson fast. Adjust and retest.

What if staff don't have capacity for another experiment?
That's the point. A Fix pilot is designed to *reduce* pressure, not add to it. If the team feels more burdened after week one, the lever is wrong, or it's too big.

What if leadership wants to see guaranteed ROI first?
Re-frame it: you're not spending money, you're buying insight into something that has likely plagued your organization for a while. A short experiment costs less than a single committee meeting about a major change initiative.

What if we have too many problems to know where to start?
This should have been clarified in the Find phase. If alignment and buy-in weren't established there, rerun Find before moving forward. You don't start Fix until the team agrees on which constraint matters most.

How to Run the FIX Mechanism

The goal: run a small, fast experiment to test whether one chosen lever actually resolves the constraint. Think of it as your minimum viable change.

Step1: Restate the Constraint

Use the same framing introduced in the Find phase:

We can't _____ because _____

This simple cause-and-effect statement anchors focus on both the constraint and its impact. For example: *"We can't reduce wait times because scheduling is manual and fragmented."* By restating it this way, you keep the team aligned on the root issue and its consequence, ensuring every Fix experiment stays aimed at relieving the true bottleneck.

Many teams skip this step. They rush to solutions before they've defined the problem. Restating the simple cause-and-effect statement forces clarity. It separates symptoms from sources so we can get to the outcomes we need. If you need to revisit this, go back to Chapter 4.

For example, when we say "we're understaffed," it might be true. But often the real issue is time wasted on redundant steps, low-value meetings, or manual data entry. One new hire might add 40 hours of weekly capacity, but freeing just 4 hours per week for 10 existing staff unlocks 40 hours, without the added cost.

Step 2: Draft Your Menu of Levers

Consider how small levers can create out-sized results. For instance, at Good Intentions BH, a unit reduced medication errors by adding a two-minute end-of-shift checklist, while another program improved follow-ups simply by assigning one staff member to review charts for ten minutes each day. Simple, low-cost adjustments like these illustrate the essence of a lever, a targeted action that multiplies impact without adding weight.

For this step, brainstorm freely and without judgment: 3–5 ideas at a minimum, and ideally one from each of three domains (people, process and technology). This should be a creative, blind list of possibilities, not a filtered one. Treat every new idea, technique, or strategy you encounter as a potential lever you could test at some point. The key is not whether it's "good" or "realistic", it's whether it's possible to imagine testing it.

Once you've built your list, consider sharing it across teams or departments. A shared lever library becomes a living inventory of what your organization can pull when the next constraint emerges.

Domain	Sample Lever Ideas
People	Reassign staff hours, create daily stand-ups, cross-train staff
Process	Collapse steps, remove redundant approvals, simplify flows
Technology	Use automated reminders, dashboards, shared tools

3. Pick One Lever to Test

Now comes the prioritization. This may be the hardest part. You'll want to try all five ideas. Don't. Choose one based on three filters:

→ Speed: How fast can you launch it?

→ Effort: How much work, cost, or disruption?

→ Confidence: How likely is this to help with the constraint you identified?

Most leaders overestimate effort, and underestimate the payoff of a targeted test. A test that takes two weeks and no additional costs in extra tools can generate insights that would otherwise cost six months of meetings. Your goal isn't to get it right, it's to learn fast enough to know what's worth scaling.

Step 4. Design and Run a Simple Pilot Test

Define:

- **Hypothesis**: If we [do X], then metric Y will improve by Z% in T time.
- **Owner**: Who runs the pilot.
- **Metric**: One measurable indicator (e.g. wait time, throughput, errors).
- **Check-ins**: Daily or weekly 15-minute syncs to monitor progress.

Keep it small. The shorter the loop, the faster the feedback.

Step 5: Measure What Happens

At the end of 2–4 weeks:

→ Did the metric move?

→ Did the team feel relief?

→ Did a new bottleneck emerge?

Data tells you what changed. Conversation tells you why. Ask staff who are impacted: "What felt different?" Their answers will often reveal hidden dynamics, policies that don't make sense, tools that slow them down, or small wins worth doubling down on.

<u>Step 6: Adjust or Confirm</u>

→ If it worked: Move toward Serve – embed it as a standard practice or playbook.

→ If mixed or failed: Either iterate on the lever (expand, tweak, change), or go back to Find to identify the appropriate constraint.

Disclaimer: Every fix will uncover another constraint. That's a good sign. It means the system is responding. The art is knowing when to stabilize and when to keep testing.

The FIX Quick Start Template

Section	Prompts
Constraint	Describe the bottleneck in measurable terms
Lever Options	Brainstorm 3–5 levers (people / process / tech)
Select Lever	Which lever you will test and why (speed / effort / confidence)
Hypothesis	If we do X, then Y will improve by Z% in T weeks
Owner	Who leads this test?
Metric(s)	Primary metric, secondary indicators

Timeline	Start date, check-ins, end date
Risks & Assumptions	What might fail? What do we assume?
Results	Actual vs. predicted, team feedback, new constraints
Next Step	Adopt / Iterate / Discard / Pivot

The Fix template is not a form to fill, it's a conversation to structure. Use it on a whiteboard, a shared document, or even sticky notes. The format doesn't matter. The collaboration does.

A Leadership Shift

What's one area in your organization where people are working harder but getting less relief?

Can you define the constraint in one measurable sentence? And design a 2–4 week test to see if a small lever can start to release the pressure?

Start there. Don't wait for perfection or for all the resources to align. The leaders who move their organizations forward aren't the ones who plan the biggest transformations, they're the ones who *run the smallest tests consistently.*

From Fix to Serve

When a Fix works, the temptation is to declare victory and move on. But that's only half the job. Sustained change happens when a proven Fix becomes a repeatable practice, something your organization can depend on to serve reliably, without heroics.

In the next chapter, we will explore how to turn your successful experiments into embedded systems, playbooks, and rhythms that sustain momentum, with the lightest frameworks possible. Because the goal isn't just to Fix what's broken; it's to build a system that's designed to stay healthy on its own.

Design your first FIX.

Scan the QR or visit BehavioralHealthFix.com/ toolkit to get the **free** 30-day cycle planner and turn one constraint into a focused, low-risk sprint.

Chapter 6

SERVE: Keep It Fixed

Quality is not an act, it is a habit.

- Aristotle

In most organizations, the story goes something like this: a team rallies to solve a persistent issue. Maybe it's reducing intake times, improving staff scheduling, or tightening referral follow-ups. The change works beautifully for a few weeks. Relief spreads. Metrics improve. Staff feel the difference.

Then, quietly, it unravels.

It could be that the person driving the changes shifts focus to something else. Or leaves the role. Other urgent issues crop up so staff shift focus. There is a change in technology. What ever the cause, the result is the same: the problems start coming back. Intake times creep back up, schedules drift, and the same errors return. It's not that people stopped caring. It's that the change never found a home.

This cycle of improvement, relief, regression isn't unique to behavioral health. But it's particularly problematic here, where leaders are fighting burnout, turnover, and overwhelming caseloads. A 2023 study found that healthcare improvement gains often fade back toward baseline when they aren't built into reliable structures. Only 23.4 percent of programs even reported sustainability beyond five years, and discontinuation was frequently tied to poor fit (Zurynski et al., 2023).

Good Intentions BH solved a documentation bottleneck that was costing ten clinical staff nearly 20 hours a week in duplicate entry. After a series of workshops and tweaks, efficiency improved by 30 percent, saving 6 hours per week. Yet eight months later, most of the gain had evaporated. Why? It existed in memory, not in a mechanism. Staff turnover, new software, and shifting priorities quickly washed the gains away.

At Amazon Web Services, I learned the opposite pattern. Wins didn't drift, they accumulated by design. When something worked, it became a mechanism: a tenet, a tool, or cadence woven into existing rhythms. Ownership was clear. Inspection was predictable. And iteration was built in. The result wasn't rigidity, it was resilience. Teams could evolve fast without losing what already worked. And this was not only encouraged, it was expected.

A similar pattern was observed by the Health Foundation (2014), where they found that many improvement pilots struggle to become routine practice. While exact figures vary, the key difference for sustainability is not the funding, but whether the improvement is embedded into everyday work-flows, and given clear ownership (Jabbal, 2017).

The Institute for Healthcare Improvement (IHI) calls this the "Reliability Gap": the distance between doing something once and doing it reliably every time, and outlines that clos-ing this gap takes deliberate effort (Resar, 2006). In behavioral health, that gap widens quickly because of chronic workforce shortages, loss of institutional knowledge, shifting payer rules, and the emotional toll of care work. When everyone is stretched thin, the lightest system wins.

Relief becomes resilience only when the fix becomes part of a system. Without that translation, even the best ideas fade into the next cycle of urgency.

That's why the third part of this framework, Serve, exists. It's about building systems that keep the fix fixed. The Serve Loop converts these wins into reliable results, without adding bureaucracy or heavy processes. It's the lightest structure pos-sible to protect what's working.

Because in our work, sustainability isn't just a luxury, it's survival.

Mini-FAQ: Your First Objections

What if this adds more bureaucracy?
The Serve loop is deliberately designed to be light. Each element should take minutes, not hours. It's a rhythm check, not a paperwork generator. If it feels heavy, it doesn't Serve. It's noise.

What if staff are too busy to keep reviewing?
Serve works because it embeds into existing practices. You don't add time; you re-purpose it. Five minutes of reflection saves hours of redundant work later.

What if stakeholders see this as extra work?
Frame it as protection, not expansion. Serve protects gains that already took effort to achieve. Without it, that effort fades, and the same issues return.

What if we can't measure the gains precisely?
You don't need complex dashboards. One or two simple indicators such as saved hours, completed forms, satisfaction trends tell enough of a story to confirm traction.

What if everything feels like it needs Serve?
Prioritize. Only standardize and embed the fixes that relieve meaningful constraints. Otherwise, the system becomes cluttered again.

The SERVE Loop – Foolproof your Fix

The Serve Loop is the final phase of the Find – Fix –

Serve cycle. If Find locates the constraint, and Fix experiments with a solution, then Serve is where you install what worked into the fabric of daily operations.

Each stage builds on the previous one, turning a single improvement into an adaptive loop:

1) Standardize: Capture the win before it drifts.
2) Embed: Install it where work already happens.
3) Review: Inspect its use quickly and consistently.
4) Validate: Confirm it's still delivering results.
5) Evolve: Lighten, automate, or retire what's no longer needed.

The Serve Loop transforms one-time effort into enduring value. It's what separates temporary relief from true organizational learning.

Stage	Core Question	Measurable Outcome
Standardize	What worked, exactly?	1-page playbook or checklist anyone can follow
Embed	Where does it live, and who keeps an eye on it?	Mechanism integrated into existing rhythm + 1 named steward
Review	Is it still being used?	Weekly or bi-weekly inspection ≤ 10 min
Validate	Is it still working?	Quantify gain (time, cost, or satisfaction delta)
Evolve	Can it run lighter or smarter?	Simplify, automate, or retire

It's called Serve for a reason. It doesn't demand more; it supports the work. It's a small, steady system that sustains the win.

Implementation: Putting Serve into Practice

Let's break down each stage, with cues and metrics you can use immediately.

Step 1: Standardize – Capture What Worked

Purpose: Capture the win before it drifts.

After a successful fix, don't move on. Capture the smallest repeatable version of what worked. Write a one-page play that describes:

→ The Trigger: When does this apply?
→ The Action: What do we do?
→ The Output: What's the visible result?

Strip away extra steps, fancy terminology, or conditional paths. If someone new joined tomorrow, could they follow it? That's the test.

At the NHS Foundation, a quality improvement team addressing discharge communication gaps created a one-page "discharge checklist" that clarified who completes each step, when it happens, and what triggers follow-up. The simple visual prompt reduced incomplete discharge summaries by 37 percent within six months and sustained the improvement for over a year (Health Foundation, 2016).

Metric: % of staff trained or using the new standard.
Cue: Could a new hire do this tomorrow?

Step 2: Embed – Install It Where Work Already Happens

Purpose: Make the new behavior automatic.

Great systems don't add work, they *live inside* existing ones. Add the new play or mechanism where work already happens: a daily huddle, supervision checklist, or shared dashboard.

Assign a steward, not a manager, to the practice. Their role isn't to enforce; it's to notice. They're the keeper of awareness, responsible for flagging when it slips.

The IHI found that teams embedding process reviews (the Fix) into existing huddles or supervision routines (Serve) achieved stronger and more sustained results. In a 2021 review of 39 case studies, 68 percent of organizations reported measurable improvements in team efficiency, communication, and follow-through when huddles were built into regular workflows, instead of separate activities (Pimentel et al.,2021).

Metric: % of processes with a defined steward and cadence.
Cue: Where does this live, and who will notice when it slips?

Step 3: Review – Inspect the Process

Purpose: Check use and friction, fast.

Every system drifts. The goal isn't to prevent drift, it's to catch it early and find out why. Build a quick inspection into your existing rhythm. Five minutes during a team meeting is enough.

Ask:

→ Are we still following the fix?

→ What's getting in the way?

→ What do we need to adjust?

Keep it light. No reports, no blame, just awareness. The act of reviewing reinforces the behavior.

At Amazon, teams used "mechanism reviews" in defined rhythms. Good Intentions BH, applied the same concept through five-minute check-ins. Quick validation loops prevent regression.

Metric: Review cadence held ≥ 80% of weeks.

Cue: Are we still following the Fix?

Step 4: Validate – Confirm the Outcome

Purpose: Prove the system actually delivers.

If you don't measure, you can't manage. Every Fix should have a simple before-and-after metric attached. Choose one outcome: hours saved, rework avoided, patient satisfaction improved etc.

Compare the baseline to the current state. Capture both data and stories, because in behavioral health, qualitative wins matter too. A quote from a clinician who says, "I finally have time to focus on care again," is as powerful as a metric.

A 2021 study found that teams using simple before-and-after metrics improved performance by nearly 30 percent over those relying on observation alone (Pimentel et al., 2021). Measurement doesn't just prove success, it creates it. The key is to keep metrics simple, and include the human side.

Jeff Bezos, the founder of Amazon, was known for saying that whenever data and anecdotes disagree, the anecdote is usually right.

Metric: ≥ 10–30% gain in chosen metric.
Cue: Is it solving the problem we meant to fix?

Step 5: Evolve – Keep It Alive and Light

Purpose: Adapt before it stagnates.

Every 90 days, revisit the system. Could it be simplified, automated, or retired? Complexity creeps fast. The goal isn't to preserve everything, it's to preserve what still adds value.

In behavioral health operations, the danger of process creep is real. When new tasks, hand-offs, or forms are added without regular review, complexity compounds. Research shows that layered processes increase inefficiency and trigger workarounds that erode quality over time (Davis et al., 2019; Zheng et al., 2020).

Pruning the system is what keeps it healthy. Every mechanism, no matter how useful it once was, should earn its keep. Studies show that eliminating redundant steps improves efficiency, reduces waste, and strengthens staff engagement (Brancalion et al., 2022; Endalamaw et al., 2024).

The best systems evolve. They get lighter, not heavier.

Metric: % of mechanisms simplified, updated or retired each quarter.

Cue: If this disappeared tomorrow, what would break?

From Serve to the 30-Day Cycle

Find. Fix. Serve.

That's the loop.

In reality, this loop doesn't happen once, it runs in cycles. Each 30-day implementation cycle ends with a Serve checkpoint: What's working? What's sticking? What needs to evolve?

That's how organizations compound improvement instead of restarting it. One small fix at a time. Each Serve loop sustains the last gain, freeing attention for the next constraint.

It's how behavioral health leaders can build something many organizations never achieve: momentum.

In the end, success isn't about one big change. It's about building a system that can serve your people, your patients, and your mission long after the spotlight moves on.

Make the Fix stick.

Scan the QR or visit
BehavioralHealthFix.com/
toolkit for a **free**
weekly/monthly rhythm to
keep your Fix from sliding
back.

Part III:
What Comes Next

The best way to predict the future is to design it.
— Buckminster Fuller

Chapter 7

30 Days to Relief

Start where you are. Use what you have. Do what you can.

- Arthur Ashe

The further a plan travels from the whiteboard to the front-line, the more it loses energy. The pace slows. The vision gets foggy. And what started as an exciting improvement often stalls in endless meetings or dies under the weight of competing priorities.

That's not because our people aren't capable, it's more likely because the systems we use for improvement are too big, too slow, and too political.

A 12-month initiative sounds impressive, but it often hides diffusion of responsibility. A 4-week cycle, on the other hand, forces action. It cuts through noise. It creates urgency, accountability, and momentum.

Behavioral science tells us that progress finds momentum when it's visible and achievable. In complex systems like behavioral healthcare, that means designing short loops of learning so the team can see something working before asking for more.

As the Lean movement taught manufacturing, and Agile later taught tech: progress accelerates when teams deliver in small, continuous cycles, each one a chance to learn, adjust, and improve.

In behavioral health, those small cycles are key. The field runs on compassion but operates under chronic constraint: limited funding, staff shortages, and regulatory load. That's why sustainable progress isn't one sweeping reform, it's continuous, focused loops of Find–Fix–Serve that move learning from the boardroom to the front-line, and back again.

It becomes a lightweight rhythm where teams focus on one constraint, test one Fix, and embed one improvement, every month. Over time, those small Fixes compound into systemic transformation.

The 4-Week FIND–FIX–SERVE Cycle

This cycle runs on weeks, not days, because weeks match how leaders already plan and measure. Most executives think in 5-day blocks. Meetings, pay cycles, patient throughput, so, everything naturally falls into weekly patterns.

That rhythm matters. Weekly checkpoints keep attention high but manageable. Teams can look back and forward with equal ease. So, while we call it a 30-Day Cycle, we anchor it in 4 distinct weekly phases:

Week 1: Find

Goal: Identify one core constraint blocking a critical initiative or function, whether it's patient care, staff time, EHR inefficiencies, or access to services. Choose one focus area so the organization has a chance to learn, prove, and build confidence before scaling.

Recap: From earlier chapters, we learned that Find means tracing symptoms back to their real source. You look beyond surface metrics and find the friction that limits flow: the bottleneck.

How to Do It:

→ Go to the source: Don't guess from reports, observe the work where it happens.

→ Ask the right questions: "Where do things slow down?", "What frustrates you most?", "If you had one wish, what would you change?"

→ Map the flow: Use a whiteboard or virtual tool to trace how things are working. The slowest step is usually where you'll Find your constraint.

→ Pick one constraint: Not three, not five. One. Multiple experiments at once lead to cross-interference, small ripples that can have unknown effects on the organization.

Leadership Role: Executives should set the expectation that every 4-week cycle begins with discovery, not assumptions. Their job is to convene the right mix of people: those who live the process, those who depend on it, and those who can remove barriers. The core team doing this work should be as small as possible, and they should then tap into whoever else they may need, when they need it.

When leadership shows up at the source, trust increases; staff feel seen. And often, the real constraint isn't what was discussed in the boardroom, but obvious the moment you walk the hallways.

Week 2-3: Fix

Goal: Design and launch a small, time-bound test that relieves the identified constraint.

Recap: From the Fix phase, you know that improvement begins with a clear hypothesis: If we change X, we expect Y outcome in Z time.

How to Do It:

→ Design a lever, not a reform: Keep the test small enough to succeed or fail fast. For example, instead of rebuilding the intake process, test one scheduling change for one team.

→ Assign ownership: Every experiment needs one clear owner, someone who will coordinate, track, and report progress.

→ Establish metrics: Decide how you will measure impact: minutes saved, tasks completed, errors reduced, patients seen etc. Make it simple and visible.

→ Communicate the scope: Tell teams this is a 2-week

pilot. That framing creates permission to test without fear.

Leadership Role: Leaders should make Week 2-3 about focus and empowerment, not control. Their job is to remove road-blocks, ensure access, and help teams test fast. They set the tone for disciplined experimentation: short cycles, visible metrics, and quick feedback. Leaders also guard against overreach by asking, "What would it take for this pilot to teach us something real in two weeks?"

They approve time for testing, ensure psychological safety, and help translate wins into mechanisms during Week 4.

Weeks 4: Serve

Goal: Implement, validate, and embed the Fix, turning the experiment into a mechanism.

Recap: From the Serve chapter, we learned that mechanisms are light, repeatable systems that make success automatic. A good mechanism doesn't rely on memory or willpower, it runs because it's built into the work.

How to Do It:

→ Implement and observe: Roll out the fix in the pilot area. Track daily progress, and collect staff and patient feedback.

→ Validate results: Compare data before and after the change. Did the constraint ease? Did new bottlenecks appear?

→ Standardize: If it worked, document the new process.

Train relevant teams. Make the change part of the normal workflow.

→ Evolve: If results were mixed, refine and run again next cycle. The goal isn't perfection, it's progress in the right direction.

Leadership Role: During Week 4, leaders transition from sponsors to stewards. Their focus shifts to ensuring the Fix turns into a sustainable mechanism: that means verifying that data is collected, lessons are documented, and teams have the autonomy to refine. Leaders should facilitate reflection, helping teams by asking, "What made this work, and what do we need to protect as we scale it?"

Leaders also serve as connectors, ensuring the improvement spreads horizontally across departments, when it's ready. This prevents isolated wins and transforms them into organization-level gains.

Implementation: Making the Cycle Work Across Teams

1. Start with One Cycle, One Focus

Pick one area to test in: a program, issue, or workflow. Limit your scope. Run the full 4-week loop before expanding. Early success generates good faith, and demonstrates that this isn't another top-down initiative.

2. Create a Shared Constraint Log

Every team should maintain a visible list of discovered

constraints. It creates transparency, keeps improvements aligned, and prevents duplication. At the start of each cycle, review the log.

3. Use a Weekly Check-In Rhythm

Keep meetings short and structured to preserve focus and momentum. Use these three questions:
- → What did we learn last week?
- → What will we test this week?
- → What help do we need from leadership?

4. Leadership's Role: Remove Barriers, Not Run Projects

Executives should focus on enabling the Find-Fix-Serve cycle by providing time, resources, and psychological safety. Their role is to celebrate learning, even from failed tests. A quick failure that saves six months of planning is a win.

5. Keep Governance Light

Document learnings in a shared template, not a full report. The goal is speed, not bureaucracy. The faster insights move across teams, the faster the flywheel spins.

6. Celebrate the Wins

Every month, share one success story organization-wide such as a bottleneck removed, hours freed, frustration reduced. Recognition builds momentum and signals cultural change.

Why This Matters: The Power of Compounding Cycles

One 30-day win might seem small: saving 10 minutes here, one form there. But multiply that across teams, months, and years, and it transforms how an organization feels.

→ Year 1: 12 completed cycles = 12 tested and embedded improvements.

→ Year 2: Those 12 improvements reduce friction, freeing staff time for innovation and self-care.

→ Year 3: Continuous improvement becomes culture. Staff proactively propose, test, and refine improvements to help the organization serve better.

Short cycles protect teams from burnout and analysis-paralysis. They give staff a clear horizon and visible proof that leadership listens.

Common Pitfalls and How to Avoid Them

Too many simultaneous Fixes
Each department wants their own tests; that fragments focus and overloads shared staff. Prioritize one constraint per team per cycle.

Jumping to Fix before Find
Trying to test a solution without fully understanding the web of problems can lead to False Fixes. The Find process builds clarity, vision, and alignment. Finding before Fixing is foundational for success. Always start with Find.

Lack of ownership
Without a named owner for a Fix test, uncertainty creeps in and divides focus. A clearly named owner drives clarity and accountability from the start so the tests are focused, applied in the right direction, and yield the insights you need.

Leadership overreach
It can sometimes be tempting to override the core team's decisions with your ideas. That can cause a breach of trust, disengagement, and lackluster implementation. Instead, let teams propose their ideas, support them, and join the Find phase if you want to add relevant context and ideas into the mix.

Skipping Serve
Mechanism turns the insights and tests from Fix into sustainable change. Without embedding the practices in the Serve phase, wins evaporate.

Best Practices for Executive Alignment

1) Anchor to outcomes: Every Find-Fix-Serve cycle should tie to an outcome such as patient care, staff well-being, or operational flow. Every leader should know which outcome the cycle supports.

2) Model humility: Leaders should visibly learn alongside teams. Observe, ask, and listen. It builds psychological safety.

3) Protect focus: Shield teams from new priorities mid-cycle. Momentum dies when attention splinters. Remember, each cycle is only 4 weeks.

4) Use cross-functional reviews: Bring finance, IT, and clinical leads together in the last week of each cycle to reflect and spot inter-dependencies.

5) Reward learning speed: Celebrate the velocity of cycles completed, not just size of impact. Progress measured in loops is progress sustained.

The Flywheel Effect

At the core of this Find-Fix-Serve is a powerful flywheel effect that incorporates proven behavioral science and systems thinking. The flywheel effect is a cycle where each positive step makes the next one easier, creating momentum that accelerates over time.

As each 30-day cycle finishes, it builds momentum for the next. Find flows into Fix. Fix flows into Serve. Serve exposes new constraints. The cycle then begins again with a stronger foundation.

This is the flywheel of execution: a living system that unravels complexity into progress, one month at a time.

Build your 30-day cycle.

Scan the QR or visit BehavioralHealthFix.com/toolkit for **free** resources to map your constraint, set your focus, and run one complete Find–Fix–Serve cycle.

Chapter 8
Get More From Every Initiative

Give me a place to stand, and I will move the world.

- Archimedes

Every behavioral health organization is built on a complex network of moving parts that serve important and necessary functions. Strategic plans provide direction and set priorities for the year ahead. KPIs and dashboards offer visibility into performance and outcomes. Committees and workgroups coordinate across departments, while consultants, contractors, and vendors contribute specialized expertise when new challenges arise. Technology and EHR systems, meanwhile, form the digital backbone of modern care, allowing information to flow, documentation to be standardized, and operations to scale.

When all of these parts align, the organization becomes unstoppable. Goals transform into measurable progress, teams work in sync, and leadership plans with confidence. But when alignment slips, even small inefficiencies compound. The more capable the system, the greater the loss when its parts fail to move in harmony.

Why Great Systems Still Struggle

The reality is that each of these functions: strategic planning, KPI tracking, committee work, consulting, and technology were built to serve a specific purpose. However, none were built to continuously identify, test, and embed change to improve the ecosystem. The result is what many leaders quietly experience but rarely name: structural drag. This is often some combination of excessive collaboration, unproductive meetings, unnecessary communications, excessive rules, layers of decision making, or energy drain.

Strategic plans are written with a lot of effort, but by the time they're implemented, new bottlenecks appear. KPIs flag performance dips, but often without clear direction for resolving them. Committees coordinate well, yet struggle to translate insight into action between meetings. Consultants are brought in to solve specialized problems, only to spend half their engagement untangling basic operational misalignment. And technology, especially in behavioral health, promises transformation but frequently stalls during roll-out due to workflow mismatches and capacity constraints.

The problem isn't that these systems are broken. It's that they lack a shared operating rhythm that keeps them connected, adaptive, and aligned. Find–Fix–Serve fills that gap.

How the Multiplier Layer Works

Find–Fix–Serve acts as the connective tissue that integrates the organization's core systems. It converts strategy into action, data into insight, meetings into learning, consulting into capability, and technology into tangible results. In short, it makes every part of the organization work better, together.

When a strategic goal feels stalled, Find–Fix–Serve helps pinpoint the operational constraint blocking progress. When a KPI starts slipping, Find–Fix–Serve reveals the underlying reason, and guides a quick fix to correct it. When committees meet, Find–Fix–Serve gives them a process to test and validate ideas in short cycles, instead of debating endlessly. When consultants arrive, Find–Fix–Serve ensures the foundations are set so their expertise lands where it matters most. And when new technology is introduced, Find–Fix–Serve prepares the workflows, ownership, and capacity needed for adoption to succeed.

Existing Function	Purpose	Limitations	What Find–Fix–Serve Does
Strategic Plans	Set direction and focus	Execution lags behind intent	Converts strategic goals into 30-day cycles
KPIs &	Track perfor-	Show lagging	Uses constraints to

Dashboards	mance	data, not causes	explain what impacts metrics, and moves it in the desired direction
Committees & Work groups	Coordinate and plan	Discussion without ownership	Translates dialogue into short, testable cycles of delivering actual value
Consultants & SMEs	Provide expertise	Waste time fixing fundamentals	Clears bottlenecks so experts can focus on value-add work, and drive results
Technology Systems	Enable automation and data flow	Adoption stalls due to process misalignment	Ensures staff are able to get the maximum value out of using the technology

Strategic Growth and Capacity Expansion

Strategic plans are the driving document behind every major initiative. Most organizations spend significant time, effort, and resources annually just to see nothing happen.

Find–Fix–Serve provides a clear pathway to design and test a strategic initiative, and when it works, scale it to meet the set goals. It also helps the strategic plan stay relevant, and drives adoption across the organization.

When a particular plan or goal is stalled, Find–Fix–Serve acts as a quick diagnostic to find what's blocking the way, and resolve it. Over time, it establishes a clear organization wide rhythm to drive every strategic initiative.

Committees and KPIs: Turning Insight Into Progress

Committees and KPIs are the backbone of organizational governance. For committees, Find–Fix–Serve introduces a 30-day learning cadence. Instead of static agendas, committees Find one constraint to address between meetings, test a small Fix, and review results in the next session.

For KPIs, Find–Fix–Serve provides a clear path to action. Numbers stop being red or green; they become data stories that point to the next experiment. Leaders stop asking, "Who missed the target?" and start asking, "What constraint is holding us back?" The result is more ownership, more learning, and a culture that continuously improves. And when a KPI is not on track, they can use Find–Fix–Serve to move the needle.

Consultants: From Rework to ROI

External experts bring valuable knowledge, but too often they're forced to spend the early stages of their engagement fixing foundational issues that should have been addressed internally. Research on consulting operations shows that less than 10 percent of consultant time is spent directly collaborating with clients. The rest is consumed by internal coordination or navigating organizational barriers. Many projects under-perform because consultants are slowed down by organizational constraints and unclear ownership before meaningful progress can begin (Brandon-Jones et al., 2016).

Find–Fix–Serve clears those obstacles in advance by uncovering the root constraint that would otherwise slow the consultant's work. The result is higher-value hours, quicker wins, and stronger partnership. Consultants get to deliver what they were hired for, and staff experience the engagement as additive, not disruptive. Over time, this builds internal capability rather than dependency.

Technology: From Roll-out to Outcomes

Technology is one of the most powerful accelerators in behavioral health, but it's also one of the easiest to misfire. Across information-systems projects (EHR, EMR, Payroll, etc.), 50-70 percent fail to be implemented successfully, and 20-30 percent never meet their intended goals (Green, 2024). The causes aren't always technical, they're human. Unclear ownership, workflow misalignment, and limited staff bandwidth consistently slowed down progress (Ser et al., 2014).

Find–Fix–Serve prepares organizations for technology the way a foundation prepares for a building. Running Find–Fix–Serve cycles prior to implementation helps teams identify critical constraint to implementation/adoption, fix it within weeks, and embed a rhythm for feedback and iteration once the system goes live. That preparation ensures roll-out translates to organizational outcomes. Vendors spend less time troubleshooting. Staff training sticks. The investment produces faster returns.

When organizations take this approach, they stop digitizing dysfunction. They build readiness first and adoption follows naturally.

Looking Ahead

The Multiplier Layer changes how organizations operate now, but its real promise lies in what it makes possible in the future. As behavioral health continues to evolve, the demand for integrated, adaptive systems will only grow. Leaders who implement Find–Fix–Serve aren't just improving efficiency; they're building organizations that can learn and respond to match the inevitable pace of change.

In the next chapter, we'll look forward. We'll explore what the future of behavioral health could look like when Find-Fix-Serve becomes standard practice: where strategy, technology, and people move together, and where progress compounds across the entire organization.

Every tool works better in a system that adapts.

Make what you already have work better together.

Scan the QR or visit
BehavioralHealthFix.com/
toolkit for a **free** playbook to
connect your existing tech,
committees, and initiatives
into one operating rhythm.

Chapter 9
The Future You Can Build

The future depends on what you do today.

- Mahatma Gandhi

Before exploring what the next decade might hold, know that none of these changes will happen organically. Progress won't unfold through technology alone. It will depend on leaders prioritizing foundational changes over stopgap approaches.

The Setting

Ten years have passed. AI has transformed how humans and technology interact. Every quarter brought a new tool, a new expectation. Patients wanted faster access. Staff wanted

smoother workflows. Everyone wanted friction-less everything. And leaders had no choice but try to adapt to the
dizzying pace of change.

The leadership team at Good Intentions Behavioral
Health realized they couldn't keep reacting. They didn't need
another initiative. They needed a way to think and act differ-
ently.

So they tried one small test, a single Find–Fix–Serve cycle
focused on intake constraints. In thirty days, wait times
dropped by 30 percent. That one win earned relief and bandwidth. And with that bandwidth, they ran another cycle, then
another. Within a few years, Find–Fix–Serve wasn't a test any-
more. It was how they operated.

When they looked back, something had changed funda-
mentally. Turnover was down. Access was up. And for the first
time, staff weren't surviving; they were thriving. The community noticed it too. Online reviews from patients started
sounding like, "If you want to feel seen as an actual person,
Good Intentions BH is the obvious choice."

So when the board finally approved a re-brand, they
decided to choose a name that was both aspirational and
grounded in the experience they wanted everyone to have:
The Obvious Choice Behavioral Health Center.

The Patient's Day

A Tuesday morning, ten years from now. Alex wakes up
after another restless night and decides he can't keep waiting.
His AI companion has been helpful to talk to about the lack

of motivation and feelings of isolation. But it has also been prompting him to set an appointment to get in-person care. It's first recommendation is The Obvious Choice BH Center. Alex remembers seeing something about them recently. Maybe it was an ad mentioning same-day care and integration with AI companions. He's not sure, but he figures it's worth trying out.

He starts the intake process on his phone, answers a few questions that feel relevant. Within minutes, he is scheduled for a same-day virtual intake. "Wow," he thinks to himself, "that was just as easy as ordering my morning coffee". He's still a little anxious about the meeting, but a part of him is looking forward to it.

Later that afternoon, he meets a care coordinator who listens, asks thoughtful questions, and asks if he wants then to integrate with his AI companion to simplify the care process.

The coordinator also explains that staff at Obvious Choice BH take pride in being as helpful as possible. They flex care as needed; chat-based check-ins for quick questions and deeper human sessions when needed. By integrating with Alex's digital footprint, the team can provide care that's both informed and private. Before ending the call, they schedule Alex's first session with a clinician for the next morning. For the first time in months, Alex is feeling hopeful.

The Provider's Day

Maya starts the morning quietly. No backlog of patient notes waiting. Her AI tool has already summarized today's upcoming sessions, highlighting patient patterns and progress. There are notes from her supervisor too: reflection on what worked well yesterday, insights to improve care, and tips on technology use.

As she sips on her morning coffee, Maya reflects how different this feels. She joined Obvious Choice BH eight months ago, and everything seems to work here. And when something doesn't, they use a practice called Find–Fix–Serve to address it. She has space to focus on patient care, room to grow as a clinician, and time to take care of herself.

She has thirty minutes before her first session. Her first patient opted in to integrate his AI companion. Twelve years ago, when she was in school and ChatGPT dominated every conversation, she never imagined a future like this. Now, thanks to integrations with digital companions, she has a complete view of each patient: health records, wearable data, and context about daily patterns, supports, and gaps she can help close. It helps her create treatment plans that are both personalized and practical, with follow-up reminders built into their digital routine, and support from trusted friends and family.

Maya's first patient this morning is Alex. During the session, the EHR AI listens in to transcribe notes and assist with the treatment plan. Mid-session, it recommends a new sleep hygiene module based on the conversation and irregular patterns in Alex's wearable data. Maya glances at the suggestion but pauses when Alex describes his nights. The data might say insomnia, but his tone and body language is saying something else. There's tension there. So, Maya starts a new line of questions, and Alex mentions waking suddenly, heart racing, after a recurring nightmare. Instead of walking through bedtime routines, Maya shifts to gentle grounding, and screens for trauma triggers. She talks through the new treatment plan with Alex, integrates it with his AI companion, and sets an appointment for next week.

She feels confident in this direction; she knows that if she misses something, her supervisor will likely catch it and help. It's been a welcome change: leaders who coach instead of just coordinate. Documentation now happens almost in real time, so midday huddles focus on patterns emerging across caseloads. Supervisors facilitate and guide the learning process.

Ten months ago, Maya was spending nights buried in notes, running between sessions, and losing energy to compliance overload. Now, her time goes where it should: towards patient care, and driving better outcomes.

The Leadership Layer

What makes Maya's work-life balance possible isn't luck or technology. The leaders of Obvious Choice BH implemented Find-Fix-Serve for years to create a supportive staff experience.

Over time, their leadership style changed organically. It wasn't a goal they has set out with. But with AI managing workforce needs and service demands, daily logistics took less time. So they started going directly to staff to Find constraints they could help Fix. This became standard practice. So while the leadership team at Obvious Choice BH was still driving high-level strategy, they were able to stay grounded in the day-to-day experiences of people like Alex and Maya

Team Leaders like Maya's supervisor started their week in the flow of care. They sat in on huddles, shadowed intakes, and listened for friction. When someone said, "the process is slow," they started Find. They watched staff toggle between screens, heard their exasperated sighs, and felt the frustrations that didn't show up in performance metrics. Each observation became a constraint to address. They ran small Find–Fix–Serve cycles and celebrated every win.

Program Leaders helped scale those wins. They visited the clinics, call centers, and community partners to collect stories that gave the data meaning. They invited executives along, grounding strategic conversations in lived experience. In meetings, they connected metrics with anecdotes. Program leaders ensured the organization was Finding the true constraints and Fixing them. They amplified the impact by connecting Findings across the organization, and scaling proven Fixes.

The same mindset extended beyond clinical care. **Administrative and Support Leaders** in finance, HR, IT, and operations applied it in their own domains. HR walked the onboarding process to see where qualified candidates fell through. IT sat beside clinicians, like Maya, to watch where systems slowed them down. Finance reviewed billing friction points to understand how processes impacted care. Every department practiced this in its own context, learning to see the difference between policy intent and the reality of the people they served. This built empathy across functions and drove collaboration.

Executives now collaborated directly with every level of their organization. Each week, they spend time in the field: at virtual intakes, in team huddles, within patient advisory groups. During their time, they asked three questions: What's working? What's wearing you down? What should we fix next? Then, they acted to remove structural barriers, align incentives, and protect time. They understood that presence builds trust faster than town halls ever could.

Across all levels, leaders shared the same rhythm of learning and growth. Team leaders would Find and name constraints. Program leaders would test Fixes, and turn them into patterns and solutions. Executives removed systemic barriers to Serve across the organization. Success was now measured by how quickly a constraint was removed, and the impact it had on the people.

And the result? Patients, like Alex, moved smoothly through care. Providers, like Maya, had the time and support to provide their best care. And leaders stayed close enough to support their teams.

The Horizon: Five Forces Shaping the Next Decade

The next decade of behavioral health will be shaped by five accelerating forces: shifting patient expectations, evolving workforce realities, rapid technology growth, changing policy and payment structures, and population level disruptions. Each force demands that leaders create systems capable of adapting in real-time rather than reacting through crises.

Force 1: Patient Expectations for Instant, Seamless Care

Patients now expect the same speed and simplicity they experience in other parts of their lives. Surveys from the American Psychological Association (APA) and HHS show that delayed access leads to deterioration and dropout, while fast, low-friction starts improve engagement. The new standard will be same-day or next-day access supported by AI-assisted triage and proactive follow-up. Continuity of care will involve personalized, active supports, enabled by AI, to drive follow-through with treatment plans in the patient's everyday life.

Leaders will need to redesign intake flows and feedback loops before automating them. They will need to strengthen the foundations across the organization before layering in the technology. The real challenge will be empathy at scale: keeping the system human while meeting expectations for immediacy.

Force 2: Workforce Expectations and the New Relationship with Work

Providers and staff value autonomy, growth, and alignment over endurance. Burnout remains high, but staff are less tolerant of inefficient processes and unclear leadership.

Reports from the APA and WHO show that meaningful supervision, top-of-license work, and psychological safety directly affect retention.

AI will both strain and strengthen this relationship. On one hand, cognitive offloading and constant connectivity can dull focus and shorten attention spans; on the other, AI can reduce paperwork and surface insights that make clinicians better at their jobs. Leaders will need to teach teams to use technology as augmentation, not replacement.

Force 3: Technology Everywhere, But Not Always Helpful

The market will flood with AI-enabled products promising efficiency and insight. The risk is adoption without alignment. WHO and NIST guidance emphasize human oversight and clear governance for clinical use. Leaders will need a strategy for when to build, buy, or ignore. That means evaluating not just features, but readiness: is the culture ready to adapt workflows, retrain staff, and measure outcomes? Without a coherent vision for how leaders want to serve their patients and empower staff, organizations will drown in tools while care remains unchanged.

Force 4: Policy, Payment, and Accountability Shifts

Regulators are racing to keep up with technology and new models of care. Federal policy is pushing value-based payment, parity enforcement, and data transparency. Programs like CCBHC and CoCM have shown that aligning incentives to outcomes improves access and retention. Future funding will favor organizations that can prove measurable results, integrate behavioral and physical health, and demonstrate ethical AI use. But policies will also change depending on the political landscape. Leaders will need to build inherent capacity within their organizations to weather the headwinds, and to continue to evolve within it.

Force 5: Population Level Mental-Health Changes

AI-enabled technology, generational values, and emerging social trends are now evolving in months instead of years. Loneliness, digital fatigue, and new forms of addiction are rising. Each social and technology trend introduces new mental-health challenges while workforce and patient expectations shift, again. Leaders cannot rely on static strategies. They will need embedded rhythms that allow them to sense, test, and adapt continuously.

These five forces are not independent. They reinforce each other. Patients want speed and connection. Staff want clarity, autonomy, and purpose. Technology amplifies the potential for better care, but also creates new population level challenges, as well as changing expectations. The organizations that thrive will learn quickly. They will adapt proactively. Leaders will anticipate changes in their world, and prepare accordingly.

All of these forces, are accelerating together. The danger isn't that we fall behind. It's that we try to move faster aimlessly. Momentum without structure becomes chaos.

The Call to Action: Start the Cycle

The future won't arrive through just strategy. Or technology. It will arrive through a rhythm, embedded in the fabric of your organization.

Start with one 30 day Find–Fix–Serve cycle. Pick one constraint that slows care. Run a small test. Share what you learn. Let the practice compound.

Over time, this rhythm will become the culture itself. Every improvement will free time, strengthen trust, and build resilience.

The leaders who define the next decade won't be those who adopt the most technology. They'll be the ones who keep their organizations and their people moving forward in alignment.

One Find-Fix-Serve cycle at a time.

Build your future.

Scan the QR or visit
BehavioralHealthFix.com/
toolkit for a **free** toolkit to
start your first Find–Fix–Serve
cycle while the vision is still
fresh.

Epilogue

When I first started this journey, I wasn't planning to write a book. For years, my wife—the person who has been both my partner and my mentor—told me I should. She saw what I didn't want to see yet: that I had something worth scaling, something that could help organizations in behavioral health move forward. But I always found reasons to wait. It felt easier to stay in the lane of ideas, speaking at conferences, and offering advice from the sidelines. I convinced myself that was enough.

But every time I spoke with a leader, every time I sat with an under-resourced team trying to make things work, I felt the same frustration. I knew I could do more; we all could. Then, after presenting at a conference, I had a deep conversation with the keynote speaker, a respected leader in the field. It was energizing to talk about the opportunities we had to take better care of our staff and patients. Behavioral health organizations still have so much room for growth.

As we wrapped up the conversation, I said, in passing, "I'm looking forward to transforming behavioral health together." It wasn't planned. It just came out. But as I made my way home, it stayed with me. I realized I wasn't living up to that statement, yet. I talked about change, but I wasn't doing everything I could to drive it. That moment forced me to think about what it would take to leverage my experience and perspective, and to truly make a difference.

That was the turning point. There was no time left to waste. There would never be a perfect time for me to start.

My wife had been right all along. The only way to make a difference was to just start—to put my experience into something others could leverage. This book is the first step: my commitment to systemic change in Behavioral Health.

Some of my earliest conversations about this work came from a much more personal space. Almost a decade ago, I was venting to my wife about all of the issues I was seeing in behavioral health organizations across the country. It felt overwhelming. "And what are you planning to do about it," she asked me. I stared at her blankly, "I don't know. It's just too much…"

After a few moments of silence, she asked a critical question: "If our kids needed mental health support, would you trust the system to take care of them?"

I froze. I knew the answer was no, but I didn't want to say it out loud. To her, my silence was enough of a response. She gave me her look that said, "Well, then you know what to do next." That was my first push out of my comfort zone. I stepped up. I put in more hours. I built a team. I volunteered to run critical projects across the organization. I had to learn, on my own, principles and frameworks that helped provide better care for both our patients and our staff.

That question, "would I trust my sweet girls to the system," still fuels me today. It shapes how I think about the standards of care. It forces me to think about how intentionally leaders need to design and shape organizations that prioritize patient and staff well-being. It challenges me to envision organizations that adapt while the world shifts. It also reminds me that behind every system, people are trying their best. And these people deserve systems that work as hard as they do.

At Amazon, I learned how to translate my frameworks into enduring mechanisms; mechanisms that turn complex problems into sustainable progress. But behavioral health taught me why progress matters. Every delay, every inefficiency, every broken process affects people in a profound way. This field doesn't have the luxury of waste. It deserves tools that make work easier, not harder.

Through this book, my hope is that we can shape the future of behavioral health, together. A future where we have the time and tools to resolve anything that gets in the way of our ultimate goal: to be entrusted with someone's loved one, and immerse ourselves and our organizations in their care.

Since you have made it this far, you already believe it is possible. If you're unsure what to do next, try one Find–Fix–Serve cycle in your organization. Start small. See what shifts. Share what you learn.

This is how we move beyond accepting long-standing problems as our norm. Thinking "that's just the way we do things" doesn't benefit us. It never has. We need to dismantle these reactive systems. And we can only do that together.

Find, Fix, and Serve. Together.

With gratitude and respect,
Isamu Pant

About the Author

Isamu Pant helps mission-driven leaders make a bigger impact with the resources they already have.

Across public policy, education, behavioral health, and Amazon Web Services, he kept noticing the same pattern: passionate people, well meaning leaders, and systems that made their work harder than it should be. That realization became his focus.

In behavioral health, Isamu helped organizations untangle tech, data, and clinical workflow challenges that drained their time. At Amazon Web Services he learned how to scale that same approach through clear tenets and lightweight mechanisms, keeping even massive organizations nimble. The lesson was simple: good people don't fail, systems do.

Today, he works with leaders to remove sticky constraints, reclaim capacity, and build operations that serve both their people and their mission.

Resources and Next Steps

You've already done the hardest part: seeing opportunities with new eyes. Here are the simplest next steps to turn that vision into action.

1. Free Diagnostic + 30-Day Playbook

Scan the QR or visit BehavioralHealthFix.com/diagnostic.

- 5 minute free Find-Fix-Serve diagnostic
- Clear readout of your primary constraint
- Instant access to the free Behavioral Health Fix 30-Day Playbook to run one focused Find–Fix–Serve cycle

Start here. It's the fastest way to create real movement without adding staff or funding.

2. Bring This Work to Your Leadership Team

If you want your executive, clinical, and operations leaders aligned around one constraint — and one plan — use the Leadership Bundle.

Scan the QR or go to BehavioralHealthFix.com/leadership. You'll get:

- Copies of the book for your leadership team

- Digital tools and work-sheets
- A 90-minute Constraint Clarity Summit (Virtual)

It's the simplest way to get everyone focused on the same bottleneck. Full details and guarantee are on the site.

3. If You Want Support in the Next 30 Days

To explore a 30-day sprint for your organization:

1. Complete the diagnostic at BehavioralHealthFix.-com/diagnostic
2. On your results page, request a Constraint Mapping Call

We'll review your diagnostic, pressure-test the finding, and outline what a sprint would look like for your organization.

Call availability is limited. Priority goes to organizations with executive buy-in and urgency to make a change.

Other inquiries: resources@behavioralhealthfix.com

References

Brabson, L. A., Harris, J. L., Lindhiem, O., & Herschell, A. D. (2020). Workforce turnover in community behavioral health agencies in the usa: A systematic review with recommendations. Clinical Child and Family Psychology Review, 23(3), 297–315. https://doi.org/10.1007/s10567-020-00313-5

Brancalion, F. N. M., & Lima, A. F. C. (2022). Process-based Management aimed at improving health care and financial results. Revista Da Escola de Enfermagem Da USP, 56, e20210333. https://doi.org/10.1590/1980-220x-reeusp-2021-0333en

Brandon-Jones, A., Lewis, M., Verma, R., & Walsman, M. C. (2016). Examining the characteristics and managerial challenges of professional services: An empirical study of management consultancy in the travel, tourism, and hospitality sector. Journal of Operations Management, 42–43(1), 9–24. https://doi.org/10.1016/j.jom.2016.03.007

Buell, R. (2016, December 22). A transformation is under way at U.S. Veterans affairs. We got an inside look. Harvard Business Review. https://hbr.org/2016/12/a-transformation-is-underway-at-u-s-veterans-affairs-we-got-an-inside-look

Camilleri, J., Cope, V., & Murray, M. (2019). Change fatigue: The frontline nursing experience of large-scale organisational change and the influence of teamwork. Journal of Nursing Management, 27(3), 655–660. https://doi.org/10.1111/jonm.12725

CBHC. (2020). Behavioral Health Workforce: Administrative Burden. Colorado Behavioral Healthcare Council.

Creasey, T. (2025). Change management trends outlook: 2024 and beyond. Prosci. https://www.prosci.com/blog/change-management-trends-2024-and-beyond

Cross, R., Rebele, R., & Grant, A. (2016, January 1). Collaborative overload. Harvard Business Review. https://hbr.org/2016/01/collaborative-overload

Damschroder, L. J., Reardon, C. M., Widerquist, M. A. O., & Lowery, J. (2022). The updated Consolidated Framework for Implementation Research based on user feedback. Implementation Science, 17(1), 75. https://doi.org/10.1186/s13012-022-01245-0

Davis, M. M., Gunn, R., Cifuentes, M., Khatri, P., Hall, J., Gilchrist, E., Peek, C. J., Klowden, M., Lazarus, J. A., Miller, B. F., & Cohen, D. J. (2019). Clinical workflows and the associated tasks and behaviors to support delivery of integrated behavioral health and primary care. Journal of Ambulatory Care Management, 42(1), 51–65. https://doi.org/10.1097/JAC.0000000000000257

Dixon-Woods, M., Martin, G., Tarrant, C., Bion, J., Goeschel, C., Pronovost, P., Brewster, L., Shaw, L., Sutton, L., Willars, J., Ketley, D., & Woodcock, T. (2014). Safer Clinical Systems: Evaluation findings. The Health Foundation. https://www.health.org.uk/reports-and-analysis/reports/safer-clinical-systems-evaluation-findings

Endalamaw, A., Khatri, R. B., Mengistu, T. S., Erku, D., Wolka, E., Zewdie, A., & Assefa, Y. (2024). A scoping review of continuous quality improvement in healthcare system: Conceptualization, models and tools, barriers and facilitators, and impact. BMC Health Services Research, 24(1), 487. https://doi.org/10.1186/s12913-024-10828-0

Green, J. (2024). 10 EHR failure statistics: Why you need to get it right first time. https://www.ehrinpractice.com/ehr-failure-statistics.html

Health Resources and Services Administration. (2020). Behavioral health workforce projections, 2017–2030. U.S. Department of Health and Human Services. https://bhw.hrsa.gov/sites/default/files/bureau-health-workforce/data-research/bh-workforce-projections-fact-sheet.pdf

Heath, D. (2020). Upstream: The quest to solve problems before they happen. Simon & Schuster.

HRSA. (2024). State of the Behavioral Health Workforce. National Center for Health Workforce Analysis. https://bhw.hrsa.gov/sites/default/files/bureau-health-workforce/state-of-the-behavioral-health-workforce-report-2024.pdf

Jabbal, J. (2017). Embedding a culture of quality improvement. The King's Fund.

Jack Eastburn, Alex Harris, Neeraja Nagarajan, Jennifer Rost. (2023). Is virtual care delivering on its promise of improving access? McKinsey & Company.

McCarthy, M. (2016). Increasing physicians in hospital staff does not improve quality of care, US study suggests. BMJ, i5133. https://doi.org/10.1136/bmj.i5133

Meadows, D. (1999). Leverage points: Places to intervene in a system. The Academy for Systems Change. https://donellameadows.org/archives/leverage-points-places-to-intervene-in-a-system/

Michelle Dougherty, McGavin, R., Pilar, M., Horvath, M., & Brown, S. (2024). Health Information Technology Adoption and Utilization in Behavioral Health Settings: Final Report. U.S. Department of Health and Human Services. https://aspe.hhs.gov/sites/default/files/documents/b9f858a38ff7166052 8cf1e4b8df00fa/HIT-adoption-utilization-bh-settings.pdf

New study: Behavioral health workforce shortage will negatively impact society. (2023, April 25). National Council for Mental Wellbeing. https://www.thenationalcouncil.org/news/help-wanted/

Nigam, J. A. S. (2023). Vital signs: Health worker–perceived working conditions and symptoms of poor mental health — quality of worklife survey, united states, 2018–2022. MMWR. Morbidity and Mortality Weekly Report, 72. https://doi.org/10.15585/mmwr.mm7244e1

Olakotan, O., Samuriwo, R., Ismaila, H., & Atiku, S. (2025). Usability challenges in electronic health records: Impact on documentation burden and clinical workflow: a scoping review. Journal of Evaluation in Clinical Practice, 31(4), e70189. https://doi.org/10.1111/jep.70189

Pimentel, C. B., Snow, A. L., Carnes, S. L., Shah, N. R., Loup, J. R., Vallejo-Luces, T. M., Madrigal, C., & Hartmann, C. W. (2021).

Huddles and their effectiveness at the frontlines of clinical care: A scoping review. Journal of General Internal Medicine, 36(9), 2772–2783. https://doi.org/10.1007/s11606-021-06632-9

Reilly, S. (2023, January 19). The behavioral health ecosystem is still out of alignment. Behavioral Health Tech. https://behavioralhealthtech.com/insights/the-behavioral-health-ecosystem-is-still-out-of-alignment

Resar, R. K. (2006). Making noncatastrophic health care processes reliable: Learning to walk before running in creating high-reliability organizations. Health Services Research, 41(4p2), 1677–1689. https://doi.org/10.1111/j.1475-6773.2006.00571.x

Ross, S., & Naylor, C. (with King's Fund (London, England). (2017). Quality improvement in mental health. King's Fund.

Rowan, B. L., Anjara, S., De Brún, A., MacDonald, S., Kearns, E. C., Marnane, M., & McAuliffe, E. (2022). The impact of huddles on a multidisciplinary healthcare teams' work engagement, teamwork and job satisfaction: A systematic review. Journal of Evaluation in Clinical Practice, 28(3), 382–393. https://doi.org/10.1111/jep.13648

Ser, G., Robertson, A., & Sheikh, A. (2014). A qualitative exploration of workarounds related to the implementation of national electronic health records in early adopter mental health hospitals. PLoS ONE, 9(1), e77669. https://doi.org/10.1371/journal.pone.0077669

Shapiro, J. (2017, January 13). 3 ways data dashboards can mislead you. Harvard Business Review. https://hbr.org/2017/01/3-ways-data-dashboards-can-mislead-you

State of the Global Workplace: Understanding Employees, Informing Leaders. (2025). Gallup. https://www.gallup.com/workplace/349484/state-of-the-global-workplace.aspx

Truong, H., & McLachlan, C. S. (2022). Analysis of start-up digital mental health platforms for enterprise: Opportunities for enhancing communication between managers and employees. Sustainability, 14(7), 3929. https://doi.org/10.3390/su14073929

Wager, K. A., Lee, F. W., & Glaser, J. P. (2022). Health care information systems: A practical approach for health care management (Fifth edition.). Jossey-Bass.

You, J. G., Dbouk, R. H., Landman, A., Ting, D. Y., Dutta, S., Wang, J. C., Centi, A. J., Macfarlane, M., Bechor, E., Letourneau, J., Choo-Kang, G., Kim, E. H., Magee, C., Lang, B. J., Angelo, L., Olin, J., Frits, M., Iannaccone, C., Rui, A., … Mishuris, R. G. (2025). Ambient documentation technology in clinician experience of documentation burden and burnout. JAMA Network Open, 8(8), e2528056. https://doi.org/10.1001/jamanetworkopen.2025.28056

Zheng, K., Ratwani, R. M., & Adler-Milstein, J. (2020). Studying workflow and workarounds in electronic health record–supported work to improve health system performance. Annals of Internal Medicine, 172(11_Supplement), S116–S122. https://doi.org/10.7326/M19-0871

Zurynski, Y., Ludlow, K., Testa, L., Augustsson, H., Herkes-Deane, J., Hutchinson, K., Lamprell, G., McPherson, E., Carrigan, A., Ellis, L. A., Dharmayani, P. N. A., Smith, C. L., Richardson, L., Dammery, G., Singh, N., & Braithwaite, J. (2023). Built to last? Barriers and facilitators of healthcare program sustainability: a systematic integrative review. Implementation Science, 18(1), 62. https://doi.org/10.1186/s13012-023-01315-x